Butter, Butter

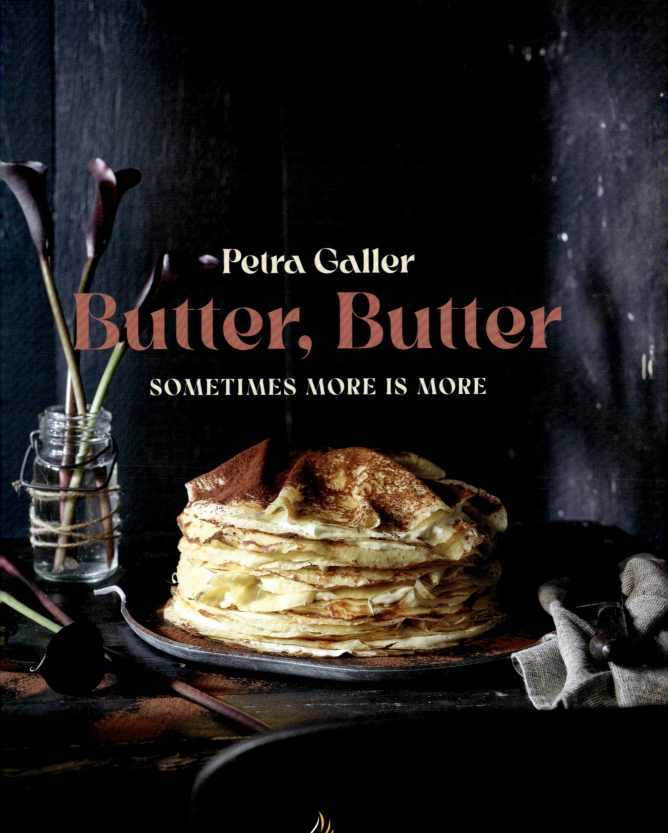

Petra Galler

Butter, Butter

SOMETIMES MORE IS MORE

ALLEN&UNWIN
SYDNEY • MELBOURNE • AUCKLAND • LONDON

To my grandmother Zaza

Contents

Introduction

The expression 'Everything in moderation, including excess' is something my father always said when we were growing up and I can't think of a better approach to sum up my style of cooking, and the way in which I strive to live. Balance is beautiful but sometimes balance in baking can be so much better when it tilts towards more.

More spice, more flavour, more crunch. Big, bold and bolshy.

I grew up in a Jewish family where the joy of preparing food and eating together is woven so deeply into our culture that dinner was always an occasion to be celebrated, and an opportunity for either me or my father to spend a couple of hours planning and prepping.

I have no doubt that this obsession stemmed from my paternal grandmother, Zaza, the original force-feeder of the family. Her savoury crêpes, Polish coffee cake (which contained no coffee at all) and her heart-attack-inducing cheesecake were legendary.

Truth be told though; these were actually the only truly delicious things she made! She wasn't a cook, in fact she strongly disliked it. It was the feeding part that was her thing, and she did that with gusto. Nothing made her happier than watching her grandchildren positively stuff themselves while she sat smiling with her white wine spritzer.

Then, and now, food has always been a form of love; the centre of all family gatherings, every holiday, every celebration. Food, at its very core, is the most nurturing gift you can offer and has the power to really connect people. There is something very personal and gratifying about cooking for someone, bringing happiness via deliciousness, turning someone's day around with something spectacular. I loved this feeling which, in hindsight, is partly what propelled me into restaurant kitchens over ten years ago.

Professional kitchens can be challenging places; an absolute hothouse of stress and tension. I was a shy and rather awkward 20-year-old, deeply unsure of myself and leaning heavily into the 'fake it til you make it' mantra. It's actually comical how little of a clue I had; it had the potential to go pear shaped quite promptly!

Despite the sheer terror I felt during these early years, I made it through, and my already sizeable food obsession only grew as I learnt more, and became more comfortable and confident. Finally I knew: I was in love with food, I knew I could cook, and I knew that this was the place for me.

The anxiety that many feel about baking is something I really hope I can ease with this book. I have never had any formal training to speak of. From a young age I devoured cook books, researched recipes and food trends for hours at a time and, although I have spent a decade working professionally as a chef, as far as baking goes, I consider myself more or less self-taught; some sort of cowboy, perhaps!

Of course, you need to pay attention to detail, and patience and precision are helpful; but baking does not need to be scary or tricky and the recipes in this book are all achievable, even for the most inexperienced baker.

Once you have a few kitchen successes under your belt, a whole world of possibility will open up and you will have the creative licence to push the limits in terms of flavour combinations, techniques and textures.

These are the recipes I have carried around with me for most of my adult life, tweaking and changing them over the years. There is a strong Middle Eastern influence woven throughout this collection, with many holding strong memories of family, discovery and sheer joy.

About six years ago, we had a family reunion in Haifa, a beautiful city in Northern Israel. We spent a month exploring the country as well as Jordan and Palestine. It was this trip where I discovered the joys of Knafeh, the power of rose water and orange blossom, and spice-spiked syrups. The food itself and the attitudes around cooking and eating really did something to me. It was so celebrated there. Walking through the spice markets in Jerusalem, seeing people from every background and walk of life coming together to enjoy the flavours, aromas and textures. It was an absolute sensory overload in the most delicious of ways and since then I have been obsessed.

There may be some recipes and flavour combinations in this book that you haven't tried before and I urge you to be bold, and experiment with something new to you. There is so much more to baking than banana cake.

Baking has always been my peace and I am beyond excited to share this book with you.

Petra

Cakes

Apple, Maple and Almond Cake

Visually, this is such a pretty cake, it just looks so charming and rustic. I'm a huge maple syrup fan and it really shines in this recipe.

The trick to getting the topping right is to use more apples than what you think you will need. You want each slice to be overlapping by half, so when the cake cooks and rises you don't have any gaps of batter peeking through.

Use a sharp knife or mandoline to slice the apples thinly, but if you're using the latter, please be careful. Every one of my fingertips have gone into a battle with the mandoline and it's notorious in commercial kitchens for being the most dangerous tool!

Preheat the oven to 160°C (315°F) fan-bake. Grease and line a 26 cm (10½ in) cake tin.

In a large frypan, melt the butter then add the cubed apples, brown sugar and cloves. Stir and cook over a medium heat until the apples have started to soften; about 4–5 minutes. Remove from the heat, set aside and let cool to room temperature.

In the bowl of a stand mixer, whisk the eggs, caster sugar and maple syrup until pale and thick.

Working by hand now, gently fold through all of the dry ingredients and currants, followed by the cooked apple and mix until just combined.

Pour the batter into the prepared cake tin, ensuring that the chunks of apple are relatively evenly dispersed. Arrange the apples slices on top of the cake, starting at the outside of the tin and working the way in, overlapping generously as you go.

Bake the cake for 75–85 minutes or until the centre of the cake feels firm to the touch. It can be a little trickier with cakes like this to tell when it is done. If in doubt, carefully insert a skewer under the layer of apples.

Allow the cake to cool completely in the tin.

Dust with icing sugar before serving, if desired.

30 g (1 oz) butter
2 Granny Smith apples, peeled and cut into 1 cm (½ in) cubes
50 g (1¾ oz) brown sugar
½ teaspoon ground cloves
4 eggs
230 g (8¼ oz) caster sugar
150 g (5½ oz) pure maple syrup
480 g (1 lb 1 oz) ground almonds
1 tablespoon ground ginger
2 teaspoons ground cinnamon
2 teaspoons baking powder
1 teaspoon flaky salt
75 g (2¾ oz) currants
4 red apples, peeled and thinly sliced into rounds
icing sugar, to dust (optional)

Blackberry, Rose and Citrus Loaf with Labneh

This is a simple little number but it's oh so effective. The texture of the crumb is tender and moist, and the tangy blackberries provide a lovely burst of sweetness.

You can swap the rose water for orange blossom and the blackberries can be changed to any berry of your choice. Regardless of any tweaks you may make, this is a beautifully balanced bake.

The frosting adds an element of interest, and makes for a lovely change from a traditional buttercream.

Labneh is strained or hung yoghurt where most of the whey is drained off so you are left with a yoghurt that has a far thicker consistency while still retaining that gorgeous tang. It is available at all good grocers or you can simply make it yourself. Line a sieve with a muslin cloth and sit it over a large bowl. Spoon the yoghurt onto the muslin and allow to sit in the fridge overnight to drain.

Preheat the oven to 160°C (315°F) fan-bake. Grease and line a 11 cm x 21 cm (4¼ in x 8¼ in) loaf tin.

Beat the butter, sugar, rose water, zests and vanilla for 3–4 minutes until pale and thick.

Add the eggs one by one, scraping down the sides of the bowl after each addition. Don't worry if the batter looks split at this point, it will come back together.

Working by hand now, gently fold through the flour, salt and ground almonds, then fold through the blackberries.

Pour the batter into the prepared tin and bake for 40–50 minutes or until the centre springs back when lightly pressed.

Allow to cool in the tin for 10 minutes before carefully turning out onto a wire rack to cool completely.

For the Labneh Frosting, combine all ingredients in a bowl and stir until smooth and combined.

Dollop the labneh on the top of the cake, smooth out with a palette knife, and dot with the extra blackberries.

150 g (5½ oz) butter, softened
170 g (6 oz) caster sugar
2 teaspoons rose water
zest of 1 lemon
zest of 1 orange
1 teaspoon vanilla paste
3 eggs
90 g (3¼ oz) self-raising flour
½ teaspoon flaky salt
120 g (4¼ oz) ground almonds
200 g (7 oz) blackberries, plus 50 g (1¾ oz) extra to garnish

Labneh Frosting
250 g (9 oz) labneh
100 g (3½ oz) icing sugar
zest of 1 lemon

Blackberry, Rose and
Citrus Loaf with Labneh

Marsala Poached Pear and Spice Loaf

This is a beautiful, rustic little number that, to me, screams autumn. The warming spices in the cake go hand-in-hand with the poached pears and it looks absolutely divine with the stalks poking up from the cake; it makes for a very pleasing cross section once cut as well.

Poached pears keep in their liquid in the fridge for up to two weeks so I would strongly recommend doubling or even tripling the recipe when you make this cake. It's always a treat to have poached pears on hand — serve gently warmed with a dollop of mascarpone or ricotta and you have an easy dessert (or dreamy breakfast) in no time.

The poaching liquid can also be reused for your next batch so whatever you do, don't throw out this liquid gold.

For the Poached Pears, place all the ingredients, except the pears, in a medium pot set over a medium heat and bring to a boil, stirring to dissolve the sugar. Add the pears and reduce to a gentle simmer. Cover the pot and cook until the pears are soft and tender, turning occasionally. You want them to be soft enough so you are able to cut them with a spoon. This should take about 40–50 minutes depending on the size of the pears.

Once the pears are tender, remove with a slotted spoon and set aside to cool before removing the core from the base with a sharp knife.

Boil the poaching liquid until it has reduced by about half and then pour over the pears. Chill until cold.

Preheat the oven to 160°C (315°F) fan-bake. Grease and line a 24 cm (9½ in) loaf tin.

For the Spice Loaf, in the bowl of a stand mixer, whisk the eggs, sugars and vanilla until pale and thick; about 3–4 minutes. With the mixer still running, slowly pour in the oil and beat until fully incorporated. The mixture may look split at this point but don't despair. Working by hand now, gently fold in all the dry ingredients followed by the chopped dates or prunes and zest.

Pour the batter into the prepared tin and then snuggle the pears into the mixture, sitting them upright. The tops of the pears should be sticking up above the batter.

Bake for 1–1¼ hours; it does take a little longer than usual because of the poached pears. When cooked, the centre should feel pretty firm to touch.

Remove the loaf from the oven and allow to cool in the tin for about 20 minutes before carefully transferring onto a wire rack.

Poached Pears

2 cups dry Marsala
2 cups water
150 g (5½ oz) caster sugar
2 cinnamon sticks
2 star anise
1 vanilla bean, split lengthways
2 long strips of orange peel
3 green Beurre Bosc pears, peeled with stems left intact

Spice Loaf

3 eggs
225 g (8 oz) caster sugar
100 g (3½ oz) brown sugar
1 teaspoon vanilla paste
225 g (8 oz) rapeseed oil
240 g (8½ oz) plain flour
1 teaspoon baking powder
½ teaspoon baking soda
2 teaspoons ground ginger
1 teaspoon ground cinnamon
1 teaspoon ground allspice
½ teaspoon flaky salt
1 cup chopped dates or prunes
zest of 1 orange

Blood Orange and Hazelnut Cake

The blood orange season is short and sweet, so every time it comes around I pounce on them. I mean, how beautiful are these creatures? The colours are so spectacular and vibrant, it's sometimes hard to believe that they are natural.

The small amount of polenta in the batter brings a gorgeous texture to the crumb of this cake, and the combination of yoghurt and ground hazelnuts ensures the moisture is kept in and the shelf life is long — win-win.

If you can't get your hands on any blood oranges, regular oranges will suffice. I've also made this using mandarins, which, I must say, could rival the original.

Preheat the oven to 160°C (315°F) fan-bake. Grease and line a 25 cm (10 in) cake tin.

Wrap the base in tin foil and place it into a baking dish. This is to catch any syrup that may leak from the bottom of the tin (so you don't have to deal with a big oven clean-up at the end).

For the Blood Orange Topping, in a pot, stir the sugar and blood orange juice over a medium heat until the sugar dissolves. Cook until thickened slightly, about 5–6 minutes. Set aside to cool.

Arrange the slices of blood orange in the base of the tin, starting at the outside of the tin and working your way in, generously overlapping as you go. Pour over the syrup and set aside.

In a large bowl, beat the butter, sugar and zests until thick and pale about 2–3 minutes.

Add the eggs one by one, scraping down the sides of the bowl after each addition.

Add the yoghurt and citrus juices and beat until just combined.

Working by hand now, fold in all the dry ingredients and gently mix.

Bake for 65–75 minutes. The centre should be relatively firm to the touch. If the cake is browning too quickly, lightly cover with tin foil.

Once cooked, allow the cake to cool for 15 minutes in the tin then turn out carefully onto a wire rack to cool completely.

Serve with a generous dollop of yoghurt.

300 g (10½ oz) unsalted butter, softened
400 g (14 oz) caster sugar
zest and juice of 2 lemons and 2 blood oranges
6 eggs
125 g (4½ oz) thick Greek yoghurt, plus extra to serve
255 g (9 oz) hazelnut meal
165 g (5¾ oz) fine polenta
150 g (5½ oz) plain or gluten-free flour
1 teaspoon flaky salt

Blood Orange Topping
220 g (7¾ oz/1 cup) caster sugar
125 ml (4 fl oz) blood orange juice
5–6 blood oranges, unpeeled, thinly sliced and seeds discarded

Burnt Basque Cheesecake

In the last couple of years, this cheesecake has seen a lot of time in the sun, and for very good reason. Gone is the humble New York cheesecake, and I can't remember the last time I made (or ate) a set cheesecake! And why would you, when you could indulge in this burnished, scorched, sexy little number?

The cake is cooked at a really high temperature, which results in its blackened exterior, creating a toasty, almost burnt butter flavour, while the middle is a just-cooked, unctuous creamy dream.

This is a recipe you will come back to again and again. It's perfectly imperfect and that's all part of the charm.

900 g (2 lb) cream cheese
375 g (13 oz) caster sugar
1 teaspoon vanilla paste
6 eggs
450 ml (16 fl oz) cream
1½ teaspoons flaky salt
130 g (4¾ oz) plain flour

Preheat the oven to 200°C (400°F) fan-bake. Grease and line a 25 cm (10 in) cake tin. You want to use two pieces of baking paper here; the idea is to create pleats and folds when lining the tin so you are left with a rustic edge on the cake.

Place one sheet of paper over the tin, pressing down firmly to cover the base and sides. Place the second piece across the top at right angles and press down so all sides are covered. The paper needs to come up at least 4cm above the top of the tin as this cake will rise to heavenly heights when cooking, before falling back down in delicious defeat when cooling.

Place the cream cheese, sugar and vanilla in the bowl of a stand mixer and beat on a medium speed until completely smooth; about 2–3 minutes.

Increase the speed of the mixer and add the eggs two at a time until fully incorporated, scraping down the sides of the bowl every so often.

Add the cream and salt and mix until just combined; only about 30 seconds.

Sift the flour evenly over the mix and whisk by hand until the batter is smooth and silky.

Pour into the prepared tin and place on the middle rack of the oven.

Cook for 40 minutes until the top is deeply caramelised, before reducing the oven temperature to 180°C (350°F) and cooking for a further 15–20 minutes or until the cheesecake is cooked but there is still a divine jiggle in the centre.

Let the cake cool completely in the tin before carefully unmoulding and gently removing the baking paper. Serve at room temperature and cut with a hot, dry knife.

Fennel and Fig Spiced Semolina Cake

Syrup-soaked semolina cakes are a Middle Eastern classic and one of my ultimate comfort foods. I have so many fond memories of eating this style of cake in Israel and it is a recipe I make all the time.

This is a cake of many names; in Israel it is known as safra. In Turkey, revani. And in Lebanon, namoura.

Regardless of the name, and no matter where you eat this gorgeous thing, it's completely heavenly.

I've given the classic a bit of a twist here with the addition of fennel and figs, a wonderful flavour combination that you don't see enough of.

There is one golden rule when it comes to soaking a cake with syrup: hot cake and cool syrup.

Preheat the oven to 170°C (325°F) fan-bake. Grease and line a 22 cm (8½ in) cake tin.

Combine the figs with all of the dry ingredients, mixing so the fruit is coated. This will keep the figs from clumping together in the batter. Set aside.

In a large bowl, beat the butter, sugar, zest and vanilla until pale and fluffy; about 2–3 minutes.

Add the eggs one by one, scraping down the sides of the bowl after each addition.

Working by hand now, gently fold in the buttermilk and citrus juice followed by the dry ingredients.

Pour into the prepared tin and gently press the whole almonds around the outer edge of the cake. Bake for 45–50 minutes or until the centre springs back when lightly pressed.

While the cake is cooking make the Lemon Syrup.

Combine all the ingredients in a small pot and stir over a medium heat until the sugar has dissolved. Bring to a gentle boil and simmer for 2–3 minutes until slightly thickened. Remove from the heat and allow to cool to room temperature.

When the cake is cooked, pierce the top all over with a skewer and drench it with the syrup. It may look like the cake is drowning for a minute here, but it will soak it all up like a sponge and the end result is positively sumptuous.

Allow the cake to cool completely in the tin before serving with a generous dollop of Greek yoghurt.

130 g (4¾ oz) dried figs, thinly sliced
2 teaspoons baking powder
200 g (7 oz) fine semolina
180 g (6¼ oz) ground almonds
½ teaspoon flaky salt
4 teaspoons roasted fennel seeds, ground
220 g (7¾ oz) softened butter
200 g (7 oz) caster sugar
finely grated zest and juice of 1 lemon and 1 orange
1 teaspoon vanilla paste
4 eggs
125 ml (4 fl oz/½ cup) buttermilk
whole blanched almonds, to decorate
Greek yoghurt, to serve

Lemon Syrup
3 pieces of lemon rind
170 g (6 oz) caster sugar
170 ml (5½ fl oz) water

Honey Polenta Cake with Candied Fennel

Serves 12–14
generously

For quite some time, this was my breakfast cake. I would often start work a fair few hours before my fellow chefs and, as much as I adore them all, those quiet hours before the sun came up were my favourite in the day. With the whole kitchen to myself, I would slouch over my bench and write my prep list for the day while shovelling in a slab of this cake. Would we call it the breakfast of champions? It's arguable!

This is one of the trustiest cakes I know. It behaves very well every bake, and is always a crowd-pleaser. The gritty texture from the polenta, and the moist almost fudge-like interior (thanks to the generous whack of butter) makes this a bit of a special one.

This recipe definitely doesn't need an icing. A drizzle of honey, coupled with the candied fennel, and you're sorted.

Preheat the oven to 160°C (315°F) fan-bake. Grease and line a 26 cm (10½ in) cake tin.

In a large bowl, beat the butter, sugar, honey, zest and vanilla until pale and thick; about 2–3 minutes.

Add the eggs one by one, mixing until fully combined. At this stage the batter may look slightly split but it will come back together.

Working by hand now, add the ground almonds, polenta, salt and baking powder and gently fold until just combined.

Pour the batter into the prepared tin and bake for 70–80 minutes until it is a deep golden brown and the centre bounces back when pressed lightly. Don't worry if the cake looks quite brown — honey caramelises faster than sugar — but if you're worried about it getting too dark, loosely cover with tin foil halfway through the bake.

Let it cool in the pan for 15 minutes before turning out onto a wire rack to cool completely.

While the cake is cooling, get onto the Candied Fennel.

In a small pot, add the sugar and water and bring to the boil over a medium-high heat. Stir continuously until the mixture becomes syrupy; this should only take 2–3 minutes. Reduce the heat to medium and add the fennel seeds, continuing to stir until the mixture crystallises; the seeds will almost look a little dry and dusty.

Quickly remove from the heat and continue to stir until the seeds have separated. Pour onto a lined tray and allow to cool.

To serve, drizzle the cake with a little honey and scatter with the candied fennel. This cake is sensational served as is, or with a dollop of Greek yoghurt.

440 g (15½ oz) butter, softened
320 g (11¼ oz) caster sugar
140 g (5 oz) honey, plus extra to drizzle
zest of 1 lemon
1 teaspoon vanilla paste
6 eggs
450 g (1 lb) ground almonds
225 g (8 oz) instant polenta
1 teaspoon flaky salt
1½ teaspoons baking powder
Greek yoghurt, to serve (optional)

Candied Fennel
3 tablespoons caster sugar
3 tablespoons water
3 tablespoons fennel seeds

26

CAKES

Chai Spiced Carrot Cake with Cardamom Cream Cheese Frosting

Confession time . . . I have always thought carrot cake needed a serious rebrand. Think about it: how often is this classic number deeply anticlimactic? It often doesn't taste like anything, let alone carrots. Honestly, I've never had time for it.

Around Father's Day a few years ago, carrot cake requests started to come in thick and fast (who knew this was every dad's favourite flavour?) and with no way to avoid it, I decided that a good dose of a chai-style spice mix was just the thing to give this cake an update. If in doubt, I always add spice and this recipe is the perfect example of how beautifully it can work.

On paper it may look like I have gone a little too heavy-handed on the aromatics but just trust me, more is more. This cake is also outrageously quick to put together; a real one-bowl wonder.

Preheat the oven to 160°C (315°F) fan-bake. Grease and line a 20 cm (8 in) round cake tin.

In a large bowl, place all the ingredients and beat together for about 2 minutes until the batter is slightly lighter in colour.

Pour the batter into the prepared tin and bake for 50–60 minutes or until the centre springs back when lightly pressed. Allow to cool in the tin for 15 minutes before unmoulding and transferring onto a wire rack to cool completely.

Meanwhile, get onto the Cardamom Cream Cheese Frosting.

Place the cream cheese in a large bowl and beat until completely smooth. Add in the icing sugar in two batches, beating continuously until light and fluffy. Scrape down the sides of the bowl before adding the zest, cardamom and salt and giving the frosting one final beating. It should be slightly looser in texture than a regular frosting.

For the Quick Candied Carrots, combine the sugar and water in a small pot set over a medium-high heat and stir until the sugar has dissolved. Bring to a boil and simmer for 3–4 minutes until slightly thickened. Add the carrot ribbons, stirring to coat. Simmer for 3–4 minutes until softened slightly. Remove the pot from the heat and drain.

Using a palette knife, evenly spread the frosting all over the top of the cake. Garnish with candied carrot ribbons and chopped pistachio nuts and dive on in; just make sure you save some for Dad!

360 g (12¾ oz) grated carrot (about 3 carrots)
360 g (12¾ oz) caster sugar
250 g (9 oz) plain flour
200 g (7 oz) rapeseed or sunflower oil
4 eggs
70 g (2½ oz) sultanas
70 g (2½ oz) pistachio nuts, roughly chopped, plus extra for garnish
2½ teaspoons baking powder
1 tablespoon ground cinnamon
1 tablespoon ground cardamom
1 tablepsoon ground cloves
½ tsp flaky salt

Cardamom Cream Cheese Frosting
375 g (13 oz) cream cheese, room temperature
350 g (12 oz) icing sugar
zest of 2 limes
½ teaspoon ground cardamom
¼ tsp flaky salt

Quick Candied Carrots
200 g (7 oz) caster sugar
150 ml (5 fl oz) water
2 carrots, peeled into ribbons

Persian Love Cake

Legend has it, there was a Persian woman who was in love with a prince. She baked him this cake, filled with magical love powers, in the hope that this would ensure a happy ever after. There are actually two endings to this tale. In the first, the plan goes off without a hitch and the lovers drive off into the sunset. In the other, and sadly far more realistic version, the gesture is brutally rebuffed and she does what every good woman does in this sort of situation and eats her feelings, i.e. the entire cake. I mean hey, we have all been there!

On a serious note, this cake is pretty spectacular. You don't see many recipes that use raw sugar and it really makes a massive difference here texturally. The combination of spices and orange blossom water almost transports you to the Middle East on smell alone. Don't be scared of the orange blossom water; it's a strong flavour but it's only perfume-like when used too liberally.

This little number is gluten-free and will keep for up to five days; not that it usually lasts that long . . .

360 g (12¾ oz) ground almonds
220 g (7¾ oz) raw sugar
210 g (7½ oz) brown sugar
120 g (4¼ oz) butter, softened
2 eggs
250 g (9 oz) Greek yoghurt
1 teaspoon orange blossom water
½ teaspoon freshly grated nutmeg
1½ teaspoons ground cardamom
½ teaspoon flaky salt
zest of 2 oranges
70 g (2½ oz) pistachios, roughly chopped
Greek yoghurt, to serve

Preheat the oven to 170°C (325°F) fan-bake. Grease and line a 20 cm (8 in) cake tin.

In a large bowl mix together the ground almonds, both sugars and butter. Using your hands, rub the mixture together until you have the texture of coarse breadcrumbs.

Spoon about one-third of this mixture into the prepared cake tin, pressing it down to form an even layer over the base; it should be about 5 mm (¼ in) thick.

Add the eggs, yoghurt, orange blossom water, spices, salt and zest into the bowl with the remaining almond mixture and mix by hand until smooth and combined.

Pour over the base and sprinkle the chopped pistachios around the border of the cake.

Bake for 45–55 minutes. The cake will colour up beautifully and the centre will have puffed up slightly and be a little firm to the touch.

Allow to cool completely in the tin.

Serve at room temperature with a dollop of Greek yoghurt.

Pistachio and Orange Cake

I fell in love with pistachios on my first trip to Italy when I was 18 and it is an affair that will no doubt last a lifetime.

I have always felt that I should have been Italian and, going on my amazing ability to inhale my body weight in pistachio gelato for 30 days straight, I think I can safely call the country my spiritual motherland.

Pistachios are everywhere in Italian baking, especially in Sicily, where the famed Bronte pistachios are grown, and this recipe really pays homage to the traditional torte from the area.

These nuts have such a gorgeous richness to them and when paired with a generous amount of orange, it makes for a pretty special flavour, not to mention a glorious-looking cake.

My crucial tip with this one is to get your hands on the best-quality, freshest pistachios available. It's a very quick recipe to put together and because of the nut meal base, the cake lasts for up to four days.

Preheat the oven to 160°C (315°F) fan-bake. Grease and line a 20 cm (8 in) cake tin.

Place the pistachios into the bowl of a food processor and pulse until ground to a fine crumb; keep a close eye on this as too much processing can cause the oils to be released from the nuts, which will form a paste. You can add 1 tablespoon of flour into the mixer to avoid this.

In a large bowl, beat the butter, sugar, zest and vanilla for 2–3 minutes, until pale and thick.

Add the eggs one by one, scraping down the sides of the bowl after each addition.

Working by hand now, gently fold in the remaining ingredients until just combined.

Pour the batter into the prepared tin.

Bake the cake for 50–60 minutes or until the centre springs back when lightly pressed. If the cake is browning too quickly, lightly cover with a piece of tin foil.

Allow to cool in the tin for 15 minutes before carefully transferring to a wire rack to cool completely.

Before serving, scatter generously with pomegranate seeds and chopped pistachios. This cake is heavenly served with a dollop of yoghurt or crème fraiche.

280 g (10 oz) pistachios, plus extra for garnish
225 g (8 oz) butter, softened
210 g (7½ oz) caster sugar
zest of 2 oranges
1 tsp vanilla paste
4 eggs
70 g (2½ oz) plain flour; can be substituted with gluten-free flour
1 teaspoon baking powder
½ teaspoon flaky salt

To garnish
arils (seeds) from 1 pomegranate
chopped pistachios
yoghurt or crème fraiche, to serve (optional)

Torta Caprese

This is it. The only chocolate cake you will ever need.

When I want a chocolate cake, I want a CHOCOLATE cake. Give me dense, rich, fudgy, smack-in-the-face chocolate cake, not its lacklustre cocoa-powder sponge cake counterpart.

Because of the ground almond base, this cake is really moist and also naturally gluten-free. If you are not an almond fan, it can be swapped for ground hazelnuts or even walnuts. It also has a phenomenal shelf life, staying damn delicious for five to six days.

A good-quality chocolate is pretty key here; I strongly recommend Valrhona Manjari, which has lovely fruity notes, but anything around 60–70% cocoa solids will work well.

Preheat the oven to 180°C (350°F) fan-bake. Grease and line a 20 cm (8 in) cake tin.

Using a stand mixer, whisk the eggs, sugar and vanilla until pale and thick; about 5 minutes. You want this mixture to double in volume.

Meanwhile, melt the chocolate and butter in a small pot over a low-medium heat, stirring constantly to make sure it doesn't catch at the bottom. Set aside to cool momentarily.

Gently fold the ground almonds, salt and cocoa powder into the egg mix, followed by the melted-chocolate mixture stirring until just combined.

Pour into the prepared tin and bake for 45–50 minutes.

Remove from the oven and gently press the top of the cake down so it falls evenly when cooling; don't be alarmed by the cracks on the top, this is what we are after.

Let the cake cool completely in the tin before gently removing; if it is still warm, it can be very delicate.

Dust with cocoa powder, cut with a hot dry knife and serve with a dollop of crème fraiche.

6 eggs
170 g (6 oz) caster sugar
1 teaspoon vanilla paste
250 g (9 oz) dark chocolate
170 g (6 oz) butter, roughly chopped
130 g (4¾ oz) ground almonds
½ tsp flaky salt
30 g (1 oz) Dutch cocoa powder, sieved, plus extra for serving
crème fraiche, to serve

Tres Leches

If I was going to describe any cake as 'naughty' it would be this one. But misbehaving is always fun so I implore you to give this recipe a try.

Tres leches is a traditional Latin American dessert that for me, has been a recipe I only started playing around with in the last year or so. If only I had cottoned on earlier!

To describe it as moist is a complete understatement. You literally drown the tender cake in a heart attack-inducing milky mixture and I have no words to describe how moreish this is.

You will need to start this recipe at least 5–6 hours (or, ideally, the previous day) before you want to indulge.

Preheat the oven to 160°C (315°F) fan-bake. Grease and line a 22 cm (8½ in) square cake tin.

In a large bowl, whisk the eggs, sugar and vanilla until pale and thick — about 2–3 minutes.

Sieve all the dry ingredients into a small bowl and then fold into the egg mixture.

Pour in the butter and using a large metal spoon, gently fold to combine, being mindful not to knock any of the air out of the batter. We don't want to over-mix here, just fold until there are no more butter streaks.

Pour into the prepared tin and bake for 25–30 minutes or until the centre springs back when lightly pressed.

Combine all the milks in a jug and whisk. When the cake is cooked, pierce holes all over the top and immediately drown with the milk mixture.

Place the cake in the fridge overnight and serve the following day with lashings of whipped cream and bitter chocolate shavings.

5 eggs

165 g (5¾ oz) caster sugar

1 teaspoon vanilla paste

225 g (8 oz) plain flour

1 teaspoon baking powder

½ teaspoon sea salt

120 g (4¼ oz) butter, melted and cooled

375 ml (13 fl oz) evaporated milk

200 ml (7 fl oz) condensed milk

250 ml (9 fl oz/1 cup) full-fat milk

To serve

whipped cream

dark chocolate (80% cocoa solids), roughly chopped

Triple Ginger and Date Bundt Cake with Thyme Caramel

If I'm being honest, there are very few cakes I don't love (ahem, banana . . . controversial, I know).

But anything with ginger gets me every time. And this beauty is brimming with it, ground, fresh and crystallised. This spicy trio combined with the sticky sweet dates is a heavenly match and ever since the first bake, it has held its place firmly in my personal top five.

There is something about the Bundt tin that makes every cake look so special, and once fully adorned with golden caramel and fresh thyme leaves, it really makes for a beautiful centrepiece.

Preheat the oven to 160°C (315°F) fan-bake. Grease and lightly flour a 26 cm (10½ in) Bundt tin. Make sure you get into every crevasse.

In a medium bowl, place the dates, baking soda and boiling water. The mixture will foam. Allow to sit for 15 minutes to soften the dates before mashing roughly with a fork. Set aside.

In a separate bowl, whisk together the flour, baking powder and salt.

In another large bowl, beat the butter, sugar, ground ginger and grated ginger for 2–3 minutes, until pale and thick. Add the eggs one by one, scraping down the sides of the bowl after each addition.

Working by hand now, add half the date mixture, folding to combine, followed by half the flour mixture. Repeat this process, then fold through the crystallised ginger.

Pour the mixture into the prepared tin and bake for 45–50 minutes or until the centre springs back when lightly pressed.

Allow the cake to cool for 10 minutes before carefully turning out onto a wire rack. Wipe out the Bundt tin and set aside.

While the cake is cooling, get onto the Thyme Caramel.

Combine all the ingredients in a medium pot set over a medium heat and stir until the sugar has dissolved and the butter has melted. Cook for 5–8 minutes or until the mixture is thick enough to coat the back of a spoon.

Pour two-thirds of the caramel into the Bundt tin.

Using a skewer, poke holes all over the top of the cake and carefully invert the cake back into the tin on top of the caramel. Poke holes in the bottom of the cake and pour over the remaining caramel.

Allow to soak for 15–20 minutes before again turning back out on to the wire rack; it's a good idea to put a tray or baking dish underneath the wire rack here so you can catch all the gorgeous caramel.

Garnish with extra thyme leaves.

250 g (9 oz) chopped dates
1 teaspoon baking soda
250 ml (9 fl oz/1 cup) boiling water
350 g (12 oz) plain flour
2 teaspoons baking powder
1 teaspoon flaky salt
110 g (3¾ oz) butter, softened
225 g (8 oz) brown sugar
2 teaspoons ground ginger
20 g (¾ oz) finely grated ginger
3 eggs
100 g (3½ oz) crystallised ginger, roughly chopped

Thyme Caramel
225 g (8 oz) brown sugar
225 ml (7¾ fl oz) cream
165 g (5¾ oz) butter, softened
1 teaspoon flaky salt
1 teaspoon picked thyme leaves, plus extra for garnish
2 tablespoons water

Upside Down Cake

How nostalgic are upside down cakes? To be frank, when I think of them, my brain instantly takes me to a rather tacky place of tinned pineapple rings, but trust me, with this recipe we are going somewhere totally different.

The cake itself is so light, almost sponge-like due to the egg whites that you whip into fluffy submission, and the polenta adds just enough gorgeous grit. The great thing about this cake is that you can use any fruit you like, which makes it a year-round delight. I've chosen tamarillos and a few raspberries here, but literally anything will work . . . just not tinned pineapple rings.

Preheat the oven to 160°C (315°F) fan-bake. Grease and line a 25 cm (10½ in) square baking tin; a round tin will also work just as well if that's all you have.

In a small pot, melt 75 g (2¾ oz) of the butter over a medium heat. Add the brown sugar and water and stir until the sugar is dissolved.

Spread the butter mixture over the base of the tin and arrange the tamarillo rounds in rows, scattering the raspberries in the gaps.

Add the dry ingredients to a bowl and mix to combine.

In the bowl of a stand mixer, beat the remaining 175 g (6 oz) butter, vanilla and 330 g (11½ oz) of the caster sugar together until pale and fluffy; about 2–3 minutes. Add the egg yolks one by one scraping down the side of the bowl after each addition.

With the mixer on a low speed, pour in half of the milk and half of the dry mix. Mix until just combined then repeat with remaining ingredients. Pour the batter into a large clean bowl and set aside.

Wipe out the stand mixer bowl then add the egg whites. Whisk the egg whites until they are starting to foam, then slowly add the remaining 30 g (1 oz) caster sugar and whisk for a further 2–3 minutes until the mix is glossy and holding its shape.

Working by hand, gently fold the egg whites into the cake batter in two lots and mix until just combined, being careful not to deflate the mixture. Spoon the mixture over the top of the tamarillos and raspberries and level out with a palette knife.

Bake for 50–60 minutes or until the centre springs back when lightly pressed. The cake should have risen beautifully.

Allow to cool in the tin for 10 minutes before carefully inverting onto a wire rack. Allow to cool to room temperature before serving.

250 g (9 oz) butter, softened
220 g (7¾ oz) brown sugar
1–2 tablespoons water
800 g (1 lb 12 oz) tamarillos (about 5) cut into 1 cm (½ in) thick rounds
70 g (2½ oz) raspberries
300 g (10½ oz) plain flour
50 g (1¾ oz) fine polenta
2 teaspoons baking powder
½ teaspoon flaky salt
2 teaspoons vanilla paste
360 g (12¾ oz) caster sugar
6 eggs, separated
285 ml (10 fl oz) milk

Walnut and Coffee Cake

Serves 12 generously

My grandma, Zaza, used to make one cake, and one cake only; the Polish coffee cake.

Every time I visited her in Wellington, it would be sitting in pride of place on the kitchen table and the Jewish grandmother-style force-feeding would ensue in a big way.

Strangely enough, there was not one ounce of coffee in her cake and, truth be told, it was occasionally a little on the dry side but because Z made it, it was perfect, and I would happily humour her by making a solid dent in it.

Making this always makes me think of her and miss her deeply; she would have loved this cake.

Preheat the oven to 160°C (315°F) fan-bake. Grease and line a 25 cm (10 in) cake tin.

In a large bowl, beat the butter, sugar and vanilla for 2–3 minutes until pale and fluffy.

Add the eggs one by one, scraping down the sides of the bowl after each addition.

Working by hand now, add all the dry ingredients, gently folding until fully incorporated.

Pour in the espresso and mix until just combined.

Pour the batter into the prepared tin and bake for 65–75 minutes or until the centre springs back when lightly pressed.

Allow to cool in the tin for 15 minutes before carefully transferring to a wire rack to cool completely.

While the cake is cooling, make the Espresso Buttercream.

In the bowl of a stand mixer, beat the butter for 1–2 minutes until completely smooth. Add the cream, coffee, vanilla and salt and mix again for 1 minute until combined. Add the icing sugar in 2 lots and beat for 2 minutes until fluffy.

Pile the buttercream on top of the cooled cake and spread out evenly with a palette knife.

380 g (13½ oz) butter, softened
380 g (13½ oz) caster sugar
1 teaspoon vanilla paste
5 eggs
380 g (13½ oz) ground almonds
200 g (7 oz) roasted walnuts, finely chopped
100 g (3½ oz) plain flour
½ teaspoon baking powder
½ teaspoon salt
125 ml (4 fl oz/½ cup) espresso, room temperature

Espresso Buttercream
225 g (8 oz) butter, softened
25 ml (¾ fl oz) cream
15 g (½ oz) finely ground coffee (instant does the trick too)
1 teaspoon vanilla paste
1 teaspoon flaky salt
375 g (13 oz) icing sugar

Milk Chocolate Cherry Layer Cake

There is an undeniable festivity that comes with a layer cake and this one is always a crowd-pleaser. Chocolate and cherry is a bit of an iconic duo in my opinion, and who doesn't like edible gold?

If time is on your side, I recommend baking the cake layers a day in advance and chilling them in the fridge overnight. Working with cold cake is always so much easier and you are far more likely to get even, clean layers when cutting them.

If this project is a one-day wonder, chill the cakes in the fridge for at least one hour before starting to assemble. I have had many a layer-cake disaster when trying to rush this cooling process and trust me, the fridge is your friend.

The cherry compote can also be made up to three days in advance and stored in an airtight container in the fridge.

For the Cherry Compote, combine all the ingredients in a medium pot and stir over a medium heat until the sugar has dissolved. Cook for 6–8 minutes, stirring occasionally, until the cherries have softened.

Remove from the heat and blitz briefly with a stick blender; be careful of hot cherry juice flying! You want to leave it a bit textural, like a chunky jam.

Place the pot back on the heat and cook for a further 6–8 minutes until thick and jammy. Set aside until completely cool.

Preheat the oven to 160°C (315°F) fan-bake. Grease and line 2 x 20 cm (8 in) cake tins.

In a large bowl, beat the butter, sugar and vanilla for 2–3 minutes until pale and fluffy.

Add the eggs one by one making sure each one is fully incorporated before adding the next one, and scraping down the sides of the bowl after each addition.

In a separate bowl, add the flour, ground almonds, baking powder and salt, mixing to combine.

Add half of the milk to the butter mixture and beat slowly until combined, followed by half of the dry mix, then repeat with the remaining ingredients. Working by hand now, fold through the chopped chocolate.

Divide the batter evenly between the cake tins.

Recipe continued overleaf . . .

300 g (10½ oz) butter, softened
300 g (10½ oz) brown sugar
1 tablespoon vanilla paste
6 eggs
200 g (7 oz) plain flour or gluten-free flour
220 g (7¾ oz) ground almonds
4 teaspoons baking powder
1 teaspoon flaky salt
250 ml (9 fl oz/1 cup) milk
220 g (7¾ oz) milk chocolate, roughly chopped

Cherry Compote
450 g (1 lb) cherries
100 g (3½ oz) caster sugar
12 g (¼ oz) cornflour
1 tablespoon lemon juice
60 ml (2 fl oz/¼ cup) water

Sour Cream Frosting
160 g (5¾ oz) butter, softened
240 g (8½ oz) sour cream, softened
½ teaspoon flaky salt
2 teaspoons vanilla paste
1110 g (2 lb 6¾ oz) icing sugar

To decorate
edible gold leaf

Bake for 40–50 minutes or until the centre springs back when gently pressed. If the cakes are colouring too quickly, cover loosely with tin foil.

Cool in the tins for 10 minutes before transferring to a wire rack to cool to room temperature. At this point, wrap well in cling film and chill in the fridge for an hour or ideally overnight.

For the Sour Cream Frosting, beat the butter, sour cream, salt and vanilla in a stand mixer until smooth. With the mixer still going add the icing sugar, one-third at a time and beat until smooth and fluffy. Transfer to a piping bag; you don't need a fancy nozzle here, just cut the end off to form a 2 cm (¾ in) opening.

To assemble the layer cake, cut each cake in half horizontally using a sharp serrated knife. I often use a knife to score the cake all the way around to give me a guide before cutting in.

This is made a whole lot easier with a cold cake, so make sure you're generous with the cooling time post bake.

Place one layer on the board or plate you are planning to serve the cake on; it's heavy and a little tricky to transfer after assembling.

Pipe a ring of buttercream around the outer perimeter of the cake layer. This will act as a kind of dam to stop the cherry compote from leaking out. Spoon about one-third of the cherry compote into the middle of the cake layer and spread out evenly with the palette knife. Repeat this process with the next two layers, stacking them as straight as possible before placing the final layer on top.

Next comes the crumb coat; this is a very thin coating of buttercream spread all over the cake to seal in the crumbs and smooth out the shape. Don't worry if it looks a little on the messy side, no one will see it.

Chill in the fridge for 30 minutes before icing the cake all over with the remaining buttercream, using long gentle strokes. A hot palette knife is pretty helpful here if you're after a really clean, neat finish.

Adorn with edible gold leaf and you have yourself something rather spectacular.

Rhubarb Custard Cake

I adore rhubarb and I adore this cake. It's creamy, tangy and sweet; what more could you want? The tartness of the rhubarb is the perfect foil to the velvety smooth custard base and it's oh so pretty upon completion. Make sure the rhubarb isn't cut too small as this will make it more likely to get swallowed up in the batter.

Preheat the oven to 170°C (325°F) fan-bake. Grease and line a 20 cm (8 in) cake tin.

Whisk the flour, baking powder and salt together in a medium bowl and set aside.

In the bowl of a stand mixer, whisk the eggs, egg yolk, sugar and vanilla until thick and pale; about 3–4 minutes.

With the mixer running on a low speed, add the butter, sour cream, rum and zest and mix until combined.

Working by hand now, gently fold through the dry ingredients.

Pour the batter into the prepared tin.

Arrange the rhubarb batons in tight lines on top of the cake; don't press them into the batter, just lay them gently on the top so they don't sink. Sprinkle with raw sugar and bake for 40–45 minutes until golden brown.

Cool in the tin for 10 minutes before transferring to a wire rack to cool completely.

160 g (5¾ oz) plain flour
¾ teaspoon baking powder
½ teaspoon flaky salt
2 eggs
1 egg yolk
325 g (11½ oz) caster sugar
1 teaspoon vanilla paste
55 g (2 oz) butter, melted and cooled
70 g (2½ oz) sour cream
4 teaspoons dark rum
zest of 1 lemon
360 g (12¾ oz) rhubarb, trimmed and cut into batons
20 g (¾ oz) raw sugar

Medovik — Honey Cake

This is such a showstopper and I implore you to give it a go — I promise it's not as hard as it may look (see image on page 54). Medovik is one of the most popular desserts in Slavic countries and one bite of this layered beauty and you will see why — it's eight gorgeous layers of incredibly moist honeyed heaven.

There are only three components to this gravity-defying cake; the ginger-spiced discs, the burnt honey icing, and a little patience. It's the perfect 'rainy afternoon project' bake and worth every minute of effort.

Be aware that it must sit in the fridge overnight before serving; this is so the layers have time to soften and soak up all the gorgeous burnt honey icing.

For the Burnt Honey Icing, put the honey into a small pot and cook over a medium heat for 5–6 minutes or until it turns a couple of shades darker.

Remove the pot from the heat and pour in 150 ml (5 fl oz) of the cream and the salt. Pour this mixture into a small bowl, cover and set aside in the fridge until fully cooled.

Next, get onto the Honey Syrup. Combine the honey and water in a small pot and bring to a gentle boil. Simmer for 2–3 minutes until slightly thickened. Remove from the heat and allow to cool completely.

Preheat the oven to 180°C (350°F) fan-bake. Grease and line as many baking trays as you can fit into the oven at one time. Draw a 23 cm (9 in) diameter circle on the back of each piece of paper — this will act as a template for the cake layers.

For the Cake Layers, put the butter, honey and sugar into a large pan, and cook for 5 minutes over a medium heat, or until everything is melted and the mixture is bubbling and smelling toasty.

Remove the pan from the heat and put aside to cool slightly, then pour into a bowl.

Meanwhile, in a separate bowl, whisk together the dry ingredients. Put the eggs and vanilla into a jug and whisk briefly to combine.

Begin whisking the butter mixture, slowly pouring the eggs into the bowl; make sure you keep whisking to avoid the eggs from cooking. Add in the dry ingredients and mix well with a rubber spatula until fully combined. The finished result will resemble a slightly softer and more pliable gingerbread dough.

Working while the dough is still a little warm, divide it into eight equal portions. Working with one piece at a time, put a ball of dough

Burnt Honey Icing
95 g (3¼ oz) runny honey
750 ml (26 fl oz/3 cups) cream
1 teaspoon flaky salt
320 g (11¼ oz) condensed milk, fridge cold
85 g (3 oz) sour cream
150 g (5½ oz) mascarpone

Honey Syrup
120 g (4¼ oz) honey
100 ml (3½ fl oz) water

125 g (4½ oz) butter, roughly chopped
150 g (5½ oz) runny honey
125 g (4½ oz) brown sugar
500 g (1 lb 2 oz) plain flour, plus extra for dusting
1 teaspoon baking soda
½ teaspoon flaky salt
2 teaspoons ground ginger
2 teaspoons ground cinnamon
1 teaspoon mixed spice
3 eggs
2 teaspoons vanilla paste

onto one of the prepared pieces of baking paper, lightly flour and roll until it is very thin and just a little bigger than the template. The ideal thickness for the layers is about 4 mm (¼ in). Trim the dough back to the 23 cm (9 in) circle and put the trimmings aside; we will be using these a little later.

Once you have rolled out as many as you can fit in the oven at once, bake for 8–9 minutes or until slightly firm to the touch and browning slightly around the edges. The finished cakes will be like gingerbread biscuits but with a little more flexibility.

As soon as the cake layers are cooked, remove from the oven and brush them with the Honey Syrup. It's really important to do this while the layers are still hot so they soak up all the syrup.

Slide the discs onto wire racks to cool and continue until all the discs are baked.

To finish, place all the offcuts and scraps on one of the lined trays and bake for 10–12 minutes or until fully dried out and a little crisp; we want them a shade or two darker than the discs.

To complete the icing, remove the honey mixture from the fridge and mix in the condensed milk, sour cream and mascarpone. Pour into a large bowl, add the remaining cream and whisk until medium peaks form; the icing will be far looser than a traditional icing or buttercream but should be firm enough to hold its shape.

To assemble, sandwich the honey cake layers with a little of the icing; just under a ⅓ cup should do it. Make sure you are stacking them as straight as possible. Spread the remainder of the burnt honey icing over the top and sides of the cake. Chill the cake in the fridge overnight so the cake layers soak up all that gorgeous icing.

When you are ready to serve, put the baked cake scraps into a food processor and pulse to form fine crumbs. Press the golden crumbs all up the sides of the cake to garnish.

Medovik — Honey Cake

Orange and Poppyseed Bundt

Orange and Poppyseed Bundt

As a good Jewish girl, I couldn't NOT include this traditional classic.

I can't tell you how many slabs of this cake I have put away in my time and it still never loses its charm.

Because you are using the whole orange, skin, pith and all, you get a beautiful bitterness that makes for a very balanced cake; no cloying sweetness here. This can be a little dangerous as it makes it very easy to go back for seconds or thirds (or fourths).

It could not be quicker to put together and requires so few ingredients it will fast become your go-to.

Unlike a lot of recipes out there that swear on a two-hour boil time, you only need to boil the oranges here for about 30 minutes. You just need them soft enough to blitz up in the food processor. The recipe calls for room temperature orange purée, so if you are in a rush spread the purée onto a large baking tray and cool in the fridge; this should only take about 30 minutes as well.

I would advise cooking enough oranges for a couple of cakes when you make this, as the purée can be kept in the freezer for up to 3 months and the already quick process will be halved next time round!

Preheat the oven to 160°C (315°F) fan-bake. Thoroughly grease a 26 cm (10½ in) Bundt tin, making sure you get into every little corner so there are no breakages on the other side.

Place the sugar, eggs and vanilla into a large bowl and whisk until pale and thick. Allow a good 5–6 minutes for this step as this makes all the difference to the texture of the cake.

Once whipped into oblivion, add in the orange purée and fold through by hand. Then fold through the ground almonds, baking powder, cardamom, salt and poppyseeds. Be careful not to over-mix here; we want everything incorporated well but also need to keep the light airiness that we worked so hard for. Slow and gentle is the way.

Pour the batter into the prepared tin and bake for 60–70 minutes or until firm to the touch.

Allow the cake to cool in the tin for 15 minutes before carefully turning out onto a wire rack to cool completely.

For the Orange Glaze, mix the icing sugar and orange juice in a small bowl and stir well until combined and smooth; it will be a little on the thick side but that's what we are after.

Once the cake has cooled, pour over the glaze and sprinkle with extra poppyseeds.

250 g caster sugar
5 eggs
1 teaspoon vanilla paste
550 g (1 lb 4 oz) orange purée (about 3 whole oranges, boiled until softened (about 30 minutes), blitzed to a purée and cooled)
300 g (10½ oz) ground almonds
1 teaspoon baking powder
½ teaspoon ground cardamom
½ teaspoon flaky salt
40 g (1½ oz) poppyseeds, plus extra for garnish

Orange Glaze
300 g (10½ oz) icing sugar
50 ml (1¾ fl oz) freshly squeezed orange juice

Earl Grey Cake

The outrageous amount of tea I consume each day has always been a source of mild embarrassment for me. We are talking a good 8–10 cups here . . . hold the judgement. So it's only fitting I wrangled my favourite beverage into a cake.

Earl Grey has such a gorgeous flavour; floral and citrusy thanks to the addition of bergamot oil. This is amped up in this recipe by the orange zest and a little dark chocolate for good measure. It's the perfect recipe for people who aren't wild about overly sweet bakes, and is sure to be every tea-lover's new favourite.

Preheat the oven to 170°C (325°F) fan-bake. Grease and line a 20 cm (8 in) cake tin.

Place the butter, sugar, zest and vanilla in the bowl of a stand mixer and beat for 2–3 minutes until pale and fluffy.

Add the eggs one by one, beating well after each addition and scraping down the sides of the bowl to make sure everything is incorporated nicely.

In a separate bowl combine all the dry ingredients and mix well.

In another small bowl, whisk together the milk and yoghurt and add to the butter mixture, beating until just incorporated.

Working by hand now, gently fold in the dry ingredients followed by the dark chocolate and mix until just combined.

Pour the batter into the prepared tin and smooth the top with a palette knife. Bake for 30–35 minutes until a skewer emerges with a few moist crumbs on it.

Cool in the tin for 10 minutes before turning out onto a wire rack and cooling completely.

Meanwhile, get onto the Earl Grey Buttercream.

Measure out 120 ml (4 fl oz) of the cream into a small pot and add the tea leaves. Gently heat the cream until just below simmering, then remove from the heat and allow the tea to steep for 30 minutes. Strain through a fine sieve and then refrigerate until completely cool.

Once chilled, pour into the bowl of a stand mixer and add the cream cheese, mascarpone, icing sugar and the remaining cream. Whisk until you have soft-to-medium peaks.

Spread the buttercream over the cake and garnish with some extra tea leaves if desired. And don't forget to put the kettle on!

115 g (4 oz) butter, softened
200 g (7 oz) caster sugar
zest of 1 orange
1 teaspoon vanilla paste
2 eggs
190 g (6¾ oz) plain flour
1 tablespoon Earl Grey tea leaves
1 teaspoon baking powder
½ teaspoon flaky salt
60 ml (2 fl oz/¼ cup) milk
60 ml (2 fl oz/¼ cup) Greek yoghurt
55 g (2 oz) dark chocolate, roughly chopped

Earl Grey Buttercream
180 ml (6 fl oz) cream
1 teaspoon Earl Grey tea leaves, extra for garnish
130 g (4¾ oz) cream cheese, softened
50 g (1¾ oz) mascarpone, room temperature
40 g (1½ oz) icing sugar

Black Sesame Cake

Black sesame is such a gorgeous flavour. Nuttier and richer than its blonde counterpart, when used in large quantities you get a really beautiful earthiness and this recipe really lets those little seeds shine.

The yoghurt helps to keep the crumb lovely and moist as well as making sure the sweetness is kept in check. It's a rather striking, Tim Burton-esque bake and something a little bit different.

Preheat the oven to 175°C (335°F) fan-bake. Grease and line a 20 cm (8 in) cake tin.

Place the sesame seeds and honey in the bowl of a food processor or spice grinder and blend until a rough paste forms; give this about 1–2 minutes. Don't worry about getting it super smooth, a little texture is good. Scrape into a small bowl, add the yoghurt and mix to combine. Set aside.

In the bowl of a stand mixer, whisk the eggs, sugar and vanilla until pale and thick. Add the oil in a steady stream and whisk until homogenous.

In a separate bowl, mix together all the dry ingredients.

Working by hand now, gently mix half of the black sesame mixture through the egg mixture until just combined. Follow with half of the dry ingredients, then repeat with the remaining ingredients. Be mindful not to over-mix.

Pour the batter into the prepared tin, smoothing the top with a palette knife. Bake the cake for 30–35 minutes, or until a skewer comes out clean.

Cool in the tin for 10 minutes before turning out onto a wire rack to cool completely.

For the Black Sesame Buttercream, beat the butter until completely smooth. Add the icing sugar, salt and sesame seeds and mix until combined. Drizzle in the milk and beat for 1–2 minutes until smooth and creamy.

When the cake is completely cool, generously slather on the buttercream with the palette knife and garnish with extra sesame seeds.

The cake will keep for 2–3 days in an airtight container at room temperature.

125 g (4½ oz) black sesame seeds, toasted
15 g (½ oz) honey
140 g (5 oz) Greek yoghurt
2 eggs
225 g (8 oz) caster sugar
1 teaspoon vanilla paste
3 tablespoons rapeseed oil
1 teaspoon baking powder
¼ teaspoon baking soda
¼ teaspoon flaky salt
225 g (8 oz) plain flour

Black Sesame Buttercream
170 g (6 oz) butter, softened
300 g (10½ oz) icing sugar
½ teaspoon flaky salt
60 g (2¼ oz) black sesame seeds, toasted and roughly ground in mortar and pestle, plus extra for decorating
1–2 tablespoons milk

Tiramisu Crêpe Cake

Nothing screams breakfast louder than coffee and crêpes, so if you have ever needed a plausible excuse to roll out of bed and start the day with cake, then look no further.

Making 30 crêpes may seem a little excessive but trust me, it is oh so worth it, and you will be delighted with the multi-layered final result. It really is a rather simple procedure once you get going, and this makes for a very impressive and crowd-pleasing centrepiece.

The crêpes and the tiramisu filling can both be made a day in advance; just make sure the crêpes are tightly wrapped at room temperature and the filling is kept refrigerated until needed.

To make the crêpe batter, combine all the ingredients in a large bowl and whisk thoroughly until lump-free and silky. I sometimes will give this a quick once-over with a stick blender to really get it super smooth. This is a pretty big batch so you will need the largest bowl you have.

Have a silicone pastry brush and the extra butter in a small bowl ready to use.

Place a 22 cm (8½ in) pan on a medium-high heat and brush with some butter.

When lightly bubbling, pour in enough batter to coat the pan; I use a ¼ cup measure, which ensures evenly sized crêpes. Tilt the pan until the base is evenly covered with the batter; you want to work relatively quickly here. Cook for about about 35–45 seconds; the crêpe is ready to flip when bubbles appear on the surface. Flip with a spatula or palette knife and cook for a further 20–30 seconds. Transfer to a plate and cover with a damp tea towel. Repeat this process until you have about 30 crêpes.

To make the filling, whisk the mascarpone, icing sugar, coffee, vanilla and brandy in a stand mixer until light and slightly thickened. Add the cream, then whisk until combined and just holding its shape.

To assemble the cake, place a crêpe on a serving board or plate and spread over a little of the filling with a palette knife. You want about 1–2 tablespoons of filling per layer; too much and the crêpes have a tendency to slip and slide a bit.

Repeat, layering crêpes and filling, before topping with the final crêpe and dusting generously with cocoa powder.

Crêpes
90 g (3¼ oz) butter, melted, plus 45 g (1¾ oz) melted to cook the crêpes
1.125 litres (39 fl oz/4½ cups) milk
450 g (1 lb) plain flour
6 eggs
30 g (1 oz) caster sugar

Tiramisu Filling
1 kg mascarpone
140 g (5 oz) icing sugar
1 tablespoon ground coffee
1 teaspoon vanilla paste
5 tablespoons brandy
200 ml (7 fl oz) cream
Dutch cocoa powder, for dusting

Fudge Ribbon Cake

My mother's good friend invented this cake. I can't remember the first time I ate this, but I was probably about six or seven years old. It featured at every get-together and family dinner and it truly is sensational. Moist, rich and naughty, I urge you to whip this up as soon as possible.

The layer in the centre isn't really a fudge so to speak, however this is what this cake has been called my whole life so we are going with it!

I love this cake ever so slightly warm as it takes on an almost pudding-like consistency in the middle. It keeps incredibly well, about 4–5 days, but I can guarantee that it will be demolished before then. I'm salivating writing this.

Preheat the oven to 180°C (350°F) fan-bake. Grease and line a 22 cm (8½ in) springform cake tin.

In a small pot, melt the butter and cocoa together on a low heat, stirring constantly.

Remove from the heat and allow to cool for a quick moment before adding the sugar. Stir well to combine; the heat from the mixture will start dissolving the sugar granules.

In a separate bowl, whisk the eggs, buttermilk and vanilla until combined. Pour into the chocolate mixture, and stir vigorously to combine, until it is thick and glossy.

Using a rubber spatula, fold through the dry ingredients until just combined.

For the Fudge Ribbon Layer, in a separate bowl, beat together all the ingredients until completely smooth.

Pour half of the cake batter into the prepared tin, then spread the fudge ribbon layer evenly on top using a palette knife. Top with the remainder of the cake batter. Smooth out with the palette knife; the chocolate mixture is really thick so running the palette knife under hot water can help to spread the batter evenly. If you are finding that too tricky, dampen your hands and gently press and drag the chocolate batter into place.

Bake for 60–65 minutes, until the centre springs back when gently pressed. It will have risen a fair bit and the top should look nice and shiny. Don't worry if there are a few cracks here and there.

Cool in the tin for 10 minutes before turning out onto a wire rack. Serve slightly warm (highly recommended) or at room temperature.

185 g (6½ oz) butter
70 g (2½ oz) Dutch cocoa powder
250 g (9 oz) caster sugar
2 eggs
125 ml (4 fl oz/½ cup) buttermilk
1 teaspoon vanilla paste
240 g (8½ oz) plain flour
1 teaspoon baking powder
1 teaspoon flaky salt

Fudge Ribbon Layer
500 g (1 lb 2 oz) cream cheese, softened
160 g (5¾ oz) caster sugar
2 eggs, whisked
1 teaspoon vanilla paste
½ teaspoon flaky salt

Mandarin, Rosemary and Olive Oil Loaf

I love baking with olive oil. It really gives such a different texture and flavour to the final product and this recipe is a pretty great example of that. This loaf is dense and super moist thanks to both the oil and the lashings of syrup it is soaked in. It's dairy-free and the plain flour can also be substituted with gluten-free flour.

We are spoilt for choice here in Aotearoa New Zealand with beautiful homegrown oils. When choosing an olive oil to bake with, especially when pairing with citrus flavours, you want something nice and zesty with grassy tones, ideally of the extra virgin variety.

Preheat the oven to 175°C (335°F) fan-bake. Grease and line a 22 cm (8½ in) loaf tin.

Put all the loaf ingredients in a bowl and mix until you have a thick batter. Pour into the prepared tin and bake for 40–45 minutes until the top is golden brown and risen, and a skewer inserted into the centre comes out clean.

While the cake is baking, prepare the syrup.

Place all the ingredients into a small pot and stir over a medium heat until the sugar has dissolved. Bring to a boil, reduce to a gentle simmer and cook for another 5 minutes. Remove from the heat and allow to cool; this will give the rosemary time to infuse, creating a gorgeously fragrant syrup.

As soon as the cake comes out of the oven, prick all over with a skewer and pour over the syrup. Leave the loaf to completely cool in the tin so it can absorb all that delicious syrup before turning out onto a serving board.

This is divine served with whipped ricotta or a dollop of yoghurt.

200 ml (7 oz) olive oil
3 large eggs
125 g (4½ oz) caster sugar
1 teaspoon vanilla paste
zest of 4 mandarins
150 g (5½ oz) plain flour
90 g (3¼ oz) ground
    almonds
¼ teaspoon salt
ricotta or yoghurt, to
    serve (optional)

Rosemary Citrus Syrup
1 large sprig of rosemary,
    leaves picked
50 ml (1¾ fl oz) lemon
    juice
50 ml (1¾ fl oz) mandarin
    juice
100 g (3½ oz) caster sugar
60 ml (2 fl oz/¼ cup)
    water

Pastry

Knafeh

On a family trip around Israel, Palestine and Jordan I think I ate my weight in knafeh. Actually, I know I did.

But it wasn't until our last stop in Amman when Nirvana was really reached.

I had heard of the hole in the wall, Habibah, and it turned out to be a mere 100 metres from our hotel, easily spotted by the hordes of people streaming from the tiny alleyway holding plates of pistachio-bejewelled, syrupy heaven.

I have forced this dish on a fair few sceptics and every time it has been met with surprised delight.

Kataifi pastry, popular throughout the Middle East and Mediterranean, is a threadlike dough, and is often referred to as 'shredded filo dough' although that is not technically accurate. Unlike filo, kataifi starts as a crêpe-like batter, which is dripped into a rotating metal plate with fine spouts. The long strands are spun out, briefly dried and cooked until you are left with vermicelli-like strings. You will find kataifi pastry at Middle Eastern and Mediterranean grocers in the freezer section.

It's crunchy, cheesy, sweet and sticky and may make little sense on paper but I implore you to try this recipe — you won't be sorry.

For the Sugar Syrup, combine the water and sugar in a medium pot and bring to the boil over a medium heat, stirring continuously until the sugar has completely dissolved.

Remove from the heat and stir in the lemon juice and orange blossom water. Set aside until cool.

Preheat the oven to 175°C (335°F) fan-bake. Generously grease a 30 cm (12 in) cast iron skillet or baking dish. Make sure you get every little corner here — nothing is more heartbreaking than a stuck knafeh.

Using kitchen scissors, roughly cut the kataifi pastry until the strands are a couple of centimetres long. Place in a large bowl and pour over the butter, tossing to ensure every strand is covered. This looks like an alarming amount of butter I know, but trust the process!

Place three-quarters of the pastry into the greased dish and press into the base and up the sides. You want to be quite firm here, almost like you are lining a tart tin with pastry. You are making the shell and you want it to be firm and compacted.

In a separate bowl, stir the cheeses, sugar, zests, salt and orange blossom water together until combined and then spread on top of the pastry base in an even layer.

Sugar Syrup
245 ml (8½ fl oz) water
400 g (14 oz) caster sugar
3 tablespoons lemon juice
1½ tablespoons orange blossom water

275 g (9¾ oz) kataifi pastry, defrosted
200 g (7 oz) butter, melted, plus extra for greasing
200 g (7 oz) grated mozzarella
200 g (7 oz) ricotta
200 g (7 oz) feta, crumbled
30 g (1 oz) caster sugar
zest of 2 oranges
zest of 1 lemon
½ teaspoon sea salt
1 teaspoon orange blossom water
50 g (1¾ oz) pistachio nuts, finely chopped
2–3 tablespoons dried rose petals, to garnish

Top the cheese with the remaining pastry, pressing down firmly again; be mindful to cover every bit of the cheese filling.

Place a piece of baking paper on top and then rest another dish about the same size on top so the knafeh is compressed.

Bake for 30–35 minutes and then remove the dish and baking paper and bake for a further 25–30 minutes until the top is golden brown and crisp.

Remove from the oven and allow to cool for 5 minutes before gently running a knife around the side of the dish.

Flip onto a platter; preferably one with sides so you avoid losing any precious syrup! You want to be brave and bold when flipping the knafeh.

Drizzle the cooled syrup all over, and allow it to soak in for 5 minutes before adorning with chopped pistachios and dried rose petals.

I absolutely insist you eat this warm.

Knafeh

Hazelnut and Plum Galette

Crust lovers rejoice, as the pastry-to-filling ratio in this recipe is very much in your favour.

A lazy cook's tart, a fruit galette is one of my go-to desserts when I'm short on time. It looks like I have put in far more work than I actually did and there is something so charming and rustic about a free-form tart like this.

This recipe uses a hazelnut pastry, which is truly delicious and incredibly well behaved, no shrinking round here.

You can swap out the hazelnuts in the pastry for almonds, and the plums can be replaced with any other stone fruit you desire.

For the Hazelnut Pastry, place the flour, sugar, salt and butter in the bowl of a food processor and pulse until the mixture resembles fine breadcrumbs. Tip this mixture into a medium bowl and, using your hands, mix in the ground hazelnuts and water. Bring the dough together with as little handling as possible. Shape into a 2 cm (¾ in) thick disc, wrap in cling film and refrigerate for 1 hour.

For the Hazelnut Frangipane, beat the butter, sugar, zest and vanilla for 3–4 minutes until pale.

Add the ground hazelnuts and salt and beat briefly to combine.

Add in the egg and beat for 1–2 minutes. The mixture should be thick and pale. Set aside at room temperature.

Preheat the oven to 180°C (350°F) fan-bake. Place an oven tray on the middle rack to heat up.

Roll the pastry out on a large and lightly floured sheet of baking paper until it is 5 mm (¼ in) thick, and then trim to form a 26 cm (10½ in) diameter circle. Using a palette knife, spread the frangipane evenly over the pastry, leaving a 5 cm (2 in) border all the way around. Arrange the plums on top of the frangipane in an even layer.

Fold the edges of the pastry over the plums, pleating as you go; warm the pastry edges up with the fingertips, as the pleating process is far easier when the dough is slightly warm and pliable.

Brush the pastry with egg wash and sprinkle all over with the raw sugar.

Slide the galette on its baking paper onto the preheated tray and bake for 50–60 minutes, until the pastry is golden brown and cooked through.

Serve hot or at room temperature, and swimming in cream.

Hazelnut Pastry
195 g (7 oz) plain flour
60 g (2¼ oz) caster sugar
½ teaspoon flaky salt
150 g (5½ oz) butter
90 g (3¼ oz) ground hazelnuts
25 ml (¾ fl oz) cold water

Hazelnut Frangipane
60 g (2¼ oz) butter, softened
75 g (2¾ oz) brown sugar
zest of 2 oranges
1 teaspoon vanilla paste
150 g (5½ oz) hazelnuts, roughly blitzed in food processor
½ teaspoon sea salt
1 egg

To assemble
10–12 plums, halved and stones removed
1 egg, beaten for egg wash
40 g (1½ oz) raw sugar
cream cheese, to serve

Cherry and Dark Chocolate Crostata

I fell into total throes of passion with crostatas when I was working as a pastry chef at an Italian restaurant in Melbourne. I was based on Lygon Street, essentially the Little Italy of the city, and you could not walk past a bakery without seeing a gorgeous rustic crostata taking pride of place. They are as timeless and famous as the tiramisu, and far more versatile.

The Italian shortcrust pastry, or 'pasta frolla', has a lovely, soft, almost cake-like quality to it. The most traditional crostata is jam-filled, usually apricot, but I have used cherries and dark chocolate here, which transform this very humble pastry into a rather decadent treat.

For the pastry, pulse the flour, sugar, zest, baking powder, salt and butter in a food processor until the mixture resembles fine breadcrumbs.

Add the egg, egg yolk and vanilla and pulse again until a shaggy dough comes together.

Tip the dough out onto the bench and bring it together with your hands, trying to handle it as little as possible. Shape it into a 2 cm (¾ in) thick flat disc, wrap it in cling film and refrigerate for 45 minutes.

Grease a 22 cm (8½ in) fluted tart tin.

Roll out about three-quarters of the pastry dough into a large circle on a floured surface until it is 5 mm (¼ in) thick. Line the tart tin by lifting up the pastry and allowing it to slump into the corners, then press lightly into the pan. Trim the edges and add them to the reserved pastry; this will be used for the lattice top. Be careful not to trim off too much pastry. We don't want it flush with the tin, rather we want the pastry to come up 1 cm (½ in) above the top of the tin. Freeze for 1 hour.

Preheat the oven to 160°C (315°F) fan-bake.

To blind bake the tart shell, spray the pastry lightly with some oil before laying 2 sheets of tin foil over the top in the shape of a cross. Gently press into the base and carefully up the sides of the tart. Fold the excess tin foil over the top of the pastry edges so all the pastry is completely covered. Fill the base of the tart with baking beans if you have some, otherwise rice or dried beans are the perfect substitute.

Blind bake for 25–30 minutes or until golden brown. Cool to room temperature.

For the filling, combine the cherries, lemon juice, cornflour and

Lemon Pastry
250 g (9 oz) plain flour
100 g (3½ oz) caster sugar
zest of 1 lemon
1 teaspoon baking powder
½ teaspoon flaky salt
150 g (5½ oz) butter, cold and diced
1 egg
1 egg yolk
1 teaspoon vanilla paste

Cherry Filling
600 g (1 lb 4¼ oz) cherries
2 tablespoons lemon juice
1 teaspoon cornflour
65 g (2½ oz) caster sugar

To assemble
65 g (2½ oz) dark chocolate, roughly chopped
1 egg, beaten for egg wash
raw sugar, to sprinkle
icing sugar, to dust

sugar in a small pot and cook over a medium heat for 4–5 minutes. The cherries should still hold most of their shape and the juice should have thickened. Set aside to cool completely.

To assemble, scatter the base of the tart with the dark chocolate before piling in the gorgeous cherry mixture.

Roll out the reserved pastry and cut into 1 cm (½ in) wide strips. Arrange in a lattice on top of the cherries. Brush with the egg wash and sprinkle with raw sugar.

Bake the crostata for 35–45 minutes; the cherries should be bubbling, and the lattice should be golden brown.

Cool in the tin for 10 minutes before carefully transferring to a wire rack to cool completely. Dust with icing sugar before serving. The crostata will keep for up to 4 days at room temperature.

Cherry and Dark Chocolate Crostata

Rugelach

Rugelach

I ate my very first rugelach at Sherman's Deli in Palm Springs many moons ago and it's been a long-standing love affair ever since.

Yiddish for 'little twists', these pastries originated in the Jewish communities of Poland and are found in every bakery across Israel.

Originally made using a yeasted dough, the cream cheese addition was an American contribution in the 1940s and, although I like to think of myself as more of a classic kind of girl, this is a twist I will gladly accept. It gives the dough a delicious tangy richness as well as making it really soft, pliable and easy to work with.

You can really play around with flavours here. For a lighter, simpler option, swap out the chocolate filling for your favourite jam or marmalade. They can also be filled with frangipane and dried fruit — anything goes.

For the Vanilla Sugar Syrup, combine all the ingredients in a small pot over a medium heat, stirring until the sugar has dissolved. Boil for 3–4 minutes until the mixture has thickened slightly. Remove from the heat and set aside to cool.

To make the Cream Cheese Pastry, combine the butter and cream cheese in the bowl of a stand mixer set up with the paddle attachment. Cream together until smooth; about 2–3 minutes. Add the remaining ingredients and mix on a low speed until a shaggy dough comes together. Tip onto a lightly floured bench and bring together with your hands, working the dough until it is velvety and smooth. Flatten into a rectangle, about 2 cm (¾ in) thick, wrap in cling film and refrigerate for 30 minutes.

While the pastry is resting, get onto the filling. Combine the chocolate and butter in a small pot and stir over a low-medium heat until fully melted. Remove from the heat and stir through all the remaining ingredients, mixing well until combined. Allow to cool; the mixture will firm up as the temperature decreases. We are looking for a spreadable thick consistency. To speed this up, pour the filling into a shallow bowl or tray and pop in the fridge for 30 minutes.

Grease and line two large oven trays.

Remove the pastry from the fridge and place onto a lightly floured bench. Roll out to a large rectangle measuring 45 cm x 30 cm (18 in x 12 in). Spread the filling evenly over the pastry using a palette knife, going right to the edges.

Using a sharp knife or pizza cutter, cut the pastry in half lengthways. Working with one half at a time, cut into triangles or wedges, with the

Vanilla Sugar Syrup
100 g (3½ oz) caster sugar
1 teaspoon vanilla paste
100 ml (3½ fl oz) water

Cream Cheese Pastry
170 g (6 oz) butter, room temperature
140 g (5 oz) cream cheese, room temperature
400 g (14 oz) plain flour
2 tablespoons white wine vinegar
¼ teaspoon baking powder
pinch of flaky salt

Chocolate Filling
55 g (2 oz) dark chocolate, roughly chopped
55 g (2 oz) butter
30 g (1 oz) cocoa
30 g (1 oz) icing sugar
zest of 2 oranges
½ teaspoon sea salt

base measuring approximately 5 cm (2 in). We are wanting to get 9 rugelach out of each half. Repeat this process with the remaining piece of pastry until you have 18 triangles. Don't worry if you have less than this; that only means you have slightly bigger rugelach, which is never a bad thing!

Starting with the longest end, roll each triangle of pastry up so you have what looks like a miniature croissant. Place the completed rugelach on the prepared baking trays, cover loosely with cling film and refrigerate for 30 minutes.

Preheat the oven to 175°C (335°F) fan-bake.

Bake the rugelach for 20–25 minutes until golden brown. Remove from the oven and immediately brush with the sugar syrup. Allow to cool on the baking trays before serving.

Mexican Chilli Chocolate Tart

This tart is truly delicious and just that little bit more interesting than the standard, with the addition of warming spice. Chilli and chocolate — an iconic duo you didn't know you needed.

Chilli increases blood flow and triggers the release of serotonin in the brain. Chocolate does the exact same thing. In conclusion, this tart will make you happy. You can't argue with science.

For the Chocolate Pastry, combine the flour, icing sugar, cocoa, baking powder, salt and butter in a food processor and pulse until the mixture resembles fine breadcrumbs. Add in the egg and egg yolk and pulse again briefly.

Tip the pastry onto the bench and use your hands to bring together and shape into a 2 cm (¾ in) thick disc. Wrap in cling film and rest in the fridge for 30 minutes.

Dust the bench lightly with cocoa powder and roll the pastry out until 5 mm (¼ in) thick. Line a 23 cm (9 in) fluted tart tin with the pastry, trimming to 1 cm (½ in) above the top. Freeze for 1 hour.

Preheat the oven to 170°C (325°F) fan-bake. Place a baking tray on the middle rack to heat up.

To blind bake the tart shell, spray the pastry lightly with some oil before laying 2 sheets of tin foil over the top in the shape of a cross. Gently press into the base and carefully up the sides of the tart. Fold the excess tin foil over the top of the pastry edges so all the pastry is completely covered. Fill the base of the tart with baking beans if you have some, otherwise rice or dried beans are the perfect substitute.

Blind bake the tart case for 20 minutes, remove the baking beans and bake for a further 10–15 minutes until the pastry is nice and dry. Remove the tart from the oven, leaving the baking tray in there, and allow to cool to room temperature.

Reduce the oven temperature to 160°C (315°F) fan-bake.

For the filling, combine the chocolate and butter in a medium pot and melt over a low heat, stirring continuously and being careful that it's not catching at the bottom. Set aside to cool momentarily.

In a large bowl, whisk the eggs, sugar, spices and vanilla until thick and pale; about 4–5 minutes.

Working by hand, fold the chocolate mixture into the egg mixture and mix until just combined. Add in the ground almonds and salt and fold until fully incorporated. The filling should be thick and glossy.

Chocolate Pastry
200 g (7 oz) plain flour
100 g (3½ oz) icing sugar
40 g (1½ oz) Dutch cocoa powder
¼ teaspoon baking powder
¼ teaspoon flaky salt
120 g (4¼ oz) butter, cold and diced
1 egg
1 egg yolk
Dutch cocoa powder, to serve
cayenne pepper, to serve

Chilli Chocolate Filling
300 g (10½ oz) dark chocolate, roughly chopped
100 g (3½ oz) butter
3 eggs
110 g (3¾ oz) caster sugar
2½ teaspoons ground cinnamon
1 teaspoon cayenne pepper
1 teaspoon vanilla paste
100 g (3½ oz) ground almonds
1 teaspoon flaky salt

Pour the chocolate filling into the tart case and spread it out evenly using a palette knife.

Place the tart back into the oven on the heated tray and bake for 20–25 minutes. The edges should be nicely set with a mischevious wee wobble in the centre.

Cool on the bench to room temperature and then refrigerate for 2–3 hours.

When you are ready to serve, dust the tart with some extra cocoa powder and cayenne pepper and slice into generous wedges using a hot, dry knife.

Mexican Chilli Chocolate Tart

Saffron Crème Brûlée Tart

Saffron Crème Brûlée Tart

Serves 8–10

This is a seriously glorious tart. Saffron doesn't tend to get a lot of attention when it comes to dessert, but its earthy, floral flavour really is stunning and visually this is a total knock-out.

While some custard tarts tend to veer on the too-sweet side, the saffron helps to give a lovely complexity to the final product and a little bit of interest.

For the pastry, combine the flour, salt, icing sugar and butter in a food processor and pulse until the mixture resembles fine breadcrumbs. Add the egg yolk and water and pulse again until the dough starts coming together in clumps. Tip onto a lightly floured surface and knead briefly until smooth. Shape into a 2 cm (¾ in) thick flat disc, wrap and refrigerate for 40 minutes.

Remove from the fridge and line a 23 cm (9 in) diameter x 4 cm (1½ in) deep fluted tart tin; trim the edges so they are 1 cm (½ in) above the edge of the tart. Freeze for 1 hour.

Preheat the oven to 180°C (350°F) fan-bake. Place a flat baking tray on the middle shelf to heat up.

To blind bake the tart shell, spray the pastry lightly with some oil before laying 2 sheets of tin foil over the top in the shape of a cross. Gently press into the base and carefully up the sides of the tart. Fold the excess tin foil over the top of the pastry edges so all the pastry is completely covered. Fill the base of the tart with baking beans if you have some, otherwise rice or dried beans are the perfect substitute.

Blind bake the tart on the hot oven tray for 15–20 minutes, before removing the baking beans and cooking for a further 5 minutes. The pastry should be a toasty biscuit colour and completely dry. Remove from the oven and allow to cool completely on the baking tray.

Reduce the oven temperature to 130°C (250°F) fan-bake.

For the Saffron Filling, toast the saffron threads in a small frypan over a high heat. This should only take a few seconds; they will darken in colour and start looking crisp. Tip them into a mortar and pestle and grind to a fine powder before transferring to a small bowl. The colour here is outrageous; almost radioactive!

Heat the milk in a small pot until just simmering and then pour over the saffron. Stir and leave to cool and infuse.

Place the egg yolks, sugar and vanilla in the bowl of a stand mixer and whisk until thick and pale. Meanwhile, heat the cream in a small pot until just below boiling point. With the mixer on a low speed, carefully pour the hot cream into the eggs and whisk until

Sweet Pastry
225 g (8 oz) plain flour
½ teaspoon flaky salt
65 g (2½ oz) icing sugar
125 g (4½ oz) butter, cold and diced
1 large egg yolk
20 ml (¾ fl oz) cold water

Saffron Filling
1 teaspoon saffron threads
100 ml (3½ fl oz) full-fat milk
6 egg yolks
50 g (1¾ oz) caster sugar, plus 20 g (¾ oz) extra for topping
1 teaspoon vanilla paste
500 ml (17 fl oz/2 cups) cream
20 g (¾ oz) caster sugar, to serve

just combined. Add the saffron-infused milk and whisk once more to emulsify. You want to keep this brief as we don't want to whisk too much air into the custard.

Strain the custard through a fine sieve into a jug, discarding any froth that may be left on top. Put the tart tin and tray back into the oven and carefully pour the custard in; this is a thousand times easier than having to transport a full tart from bench to oven, trust me on this!

Bake the tart for 45–55 minutes; the custard should be softly set with a sexy wee wobble to it. Cool on the bench before refrigerating for at least 2 hours.

Before you are ready to serve, sprinkle the sugar evenly on top and caramelise with a blow torch, moving in a circular motion until it's evenly browned. Allow the caramel to cool and set for a few minutes before slicing with a hot knife.

Ricotta, Honey and Yoghurt Tart

Ricotta and honey is an absolutely classic flavour pairing and one of my personal favourites. This tart is gorgeous, really light and beautifully silky in texture. The subtle warming spice in the pastry adds a great touch, and that flavour, coupled with the citrus zest in the filling, is a real match made in heaven.

When it comes to the ricotta, I highly recommend using a good-quality buffalo milk ricotta. It tends to be smoother and creamier than the cow's milk counterpart, with a slightly sweeter flavour.

For the pastry, combine the flour, icing sugar, spices, salt and butter in a food processor and pulse until the mixture resembles fine breadcrumbs. Add in the egg yolks and pulse again briefly. Tip the pastry onto the bench and use your hands to bring together and shape into a 2 cm (¾ in) thick disc. Wrap in cling film and rest in the fridge for 1 hour.

Dust the bench lightly with flour and roll the pastry out until 5 mm (¼ in) thick. Line a 23 cm (9 in) fluted tart tin with the pastry, trimming to 1 cm (½ in) above the top. Freeze for 1 hour.

Preheat the oven to 160°C (315°F) fan-bake. Place a baking tray on the middle rack to heat up.

To blind bake the tart shell, spray the pastry lightly with some oil before laying 2 sheets of tin foil over the top in the shape of a cross. Gently press into the base and carefully up the sides of the tart. Fold the excess tin foil over the top of the pastry edges so all the pastry is completely covered. Fill the base of the tart with baking beans if you have some, otherwise rice or dried beans are the perfect substitute.

Blind bake the tart case for 30 minutes, remove the baking beans and bake for a further 10 minutes until the pastry is dry and lightly golden in colour. Remove the tart from the oven, leaving the baking tray in there, and allow to cool to room temperature.

For the Ricotta Filling, process the ricotta, cream cheese, yoghurt, sugar, honey, zests and vanilla in a food processor until smooth. Add the eggs, and blend again briefly until just incorporated.

Pour the filling into the tart case and bake for 30–35 minutes. There should still be a slight wobble in the middle.

Cool to room temperature before setting in the fridge for 3–4 hours. Remove from the fridge at least 1 hour before serving.

Spiced Pastry

250 g (9 oz) plain flour
80 g (2¾ oz) icing sugar
¾ teaspoon ground cinnamon
¾ teaspoon ground ginger
¼ teaspoon flaky salt
120 g (4¼ oz) butter, cold and diced
3 egg yolks

Ricotta Filling

250 g (9 oz) ricotta
250 g (9 oz) cream cheese
150 g (5½ oz) Greek yoghurt
40 g (1½ oz) caster sugar
55 g (2 oz) mānuka honey
zest of 1 lemon
zest of 1 orange
1 teaspoon vanilla paste
2 eggs

Pecan Pie with Brown Sugar Pastry

It is not often that traditional American baking thrills me. I usually find the flavour profiles rather bland, just sugar on sugar. I can't say I have ever been excited by pumpkin pie, and what on earth is a snickerdoodle?

Pecan pie, however, is my one big exception. It's rich, buttery and pretty hard to stop at just one slice. I've laced mine with maple syrup and bourbon, a rather iconic duo.

Use the best-quality pure maple syrup you can find; Canadian is best but anything other than the ghastly 'maple-flavoured' syrup will do the trick.

The pastry is made using brown sugar, which really drives home the rich molasses-like flavours of this pie. Don't wait for Thanksgiving.

For the Brown Sugar Pastry, combine the flour, salt, sugar and butter in the bowl of a food processor and pulse until the mixture resembles fine breadcrumbs. Tip into a large bowl and add the egg yolk. Using your hands, work the mixture into a soft dough; don't be afraid to give it a bit of a knead to bring it together. Shape into a 2 cm (¾ in) thick disc, wrap in cling film and refrigerate for 30 minutes.

Roll out the pastry on a lightly floured bench until 3 mm (⅛ in) thick and line a 22 cm (8½ in) deep fluted tart tin. You want the edges of the pastry to come up 1–2 cm (½–¾ in) above the top of the tin. Lightly prick the base with a fork, cover again and freeze for 1 hour.

Preheat the oven to 180°C (350°F) fan-bake. Place a baking tray on the middle rack of the oven to heat up.

To blind bake the tart shell, spray the pastry lightly with some oil before laying 2 sheets of tin foil over the top in the shape of a cross. Gently press into the base and carefully up the sides of the tart. Fold the excess tin foil over the top of the pastry edges so all the pastry is completely covered. Fill the base of the tart with baking beans if you have some, otherwise rice or dried beans are the perfect substitute.

Blind bake the pastry shell for 15 minutes, before uncovering and baking for a further 8–10 minutes, until the pastry is golden and crisped.

Remove the tart from the oven, leaving the tray in there, and set aside to completely cool.

Reduce the oven temperature to 170°C (325°F) fan-bake.

Brown Sugar Pastry
150 g (5½ oz) plain flour
½ teaspoon flaky salt
50 g (1¾ oz) brown sugar
90 g (3¼ oz) butter, cold and diced
1 egg yolk

Pecan Pie Filling
4 eggs
335 g (11¾ oz) pure maple syrup
145 g (5¼ oz) brown sugar
1 teaspoon ground cinnamon
1 teaspoon ground nutmeg
1 teaspoon flaky salt
1 teaspoon vanilla paste
75 g (2¾ oz) butter, melted and cooled
2 tablespoons bourbon
210 g (7½ oz) pecans, roughly chopped, plus extra for decorating if desired

For the Pecan Pie Filling, in the bowl of a stand mixer, whisk the eggs, maple syrup, sugar, spices and salt until pale and thick; about 3–4 minutes.

In a separate bowl, combine the vanilla, butter and bourbon and whisk to bring together.

Pour this into the egg mixture and whisk again briefly to combine.

Scatter the chopped pecans evenly over the base of the tart shell. Pour the filling over the pecans; the nuts will rise to the top during the bake but if you are a big pecan fan feel free to decorate the top with some extras.

Bake the pie for 30 minutes, then cover with tin foil and bake for a further 20–25 minutes. The filling will puff up and feel quite firm to the touch when it is done.

Remove from the oven and allow to cool completely in the tin before transferring to a large plate for serving.

Pecan Pie with Brown Sugar Pastry

Rhubarb and Pistachio Tart

Rhubarb and Pistachio Tart

Even if you don't like rhubarb, you should make this just to look at it, it's just so pretty! The vibrant green frangipane emblazoned with the gorgeous pink batons is really rather striking.

This pastry recipe is a perfect starting point for those who are not too confident in crust-making. It is a total gem, very forgiving and the high fat content makes it really easy to work with. It's rather resilient, so as long as you give it a good hour to freeze before blind baking it will be on its best behaviour.

For the Shortcrust Pastry, combine the flour, sugar, salt and butter in the bowl of a food processor and blitz until it has the texture of fine breadcrumbs. Tip the contents into a large bowl.

In a separate small bowl, mix the egg yolk and cream then add to the flour mixture. Mix in with your hands, squeezing the dough together. It may look a little dry to begin but keep working it a bit and it will come together into a soft, smooth dough.

Flatten into a 2 cm (¾ in) thick rectangle, wrap in cling film and chill in the fridge for 30 minutes.

Lightly grease a 11 cm (4¼ in) x 34 cm (13½ in) x 2.5 cm (1 in) deep rectangular loose-based fluted tart tin.

When you are ready to roll, roll out the pastry on a lightly floured bench into a large rectangle, about 5 cm (2 in) bigger than the tin. Ideally, we are after 3 mm (⅛ in) thickness. Lift the pastry into the tart tin, tucking and draping making sure that it's snug against the sides. Trim the pastry so it comes up a good 1 cm (½ in) above the top of the tart tin; I often use sharp kitchen scissors for this. Freeze for 1 hour.

Preheat the oven to 160°C (315°F) fan-bake.

To blind bake the tart shell, spray the pastry lightly with some oil before laying 2 sheets of tin foil over the top in the shape of a cross. Gently press into the base and carefully up the sides of the tart. Fold the excess tin foil over the top of the pastry edges so all the pastry is completely covered. Fill the base of the tart with baking beans if you have some, otherwise rice or dried beans are the perfect substitute.

Blind bake the tart case for 30 minutes, remove the baking beans and tin foil and bake for a further 10 minutes or until the pastry is dry and lightly golden in colour. Remove the tart from the oven and set aside to cool.

Shortcrust Pastry
240 g (8½ oz) plain flour
65 g (2½ oz) caster sugar
¼ teaspoon flaky salt
140 g (5 oz) butter, cold and cubed
1 large egg yolk
50 ml (1¾ fl oz) cream

Pistachio Frangipane
60 g (2¼ oz) butter, softened
75 g (2¾ oz) caster sugar
zest of 1 orange
zest of 1 lemon
1 teaspoon vanilla paste
150 g (5½ oz) pistachios, roughly blitzed in food processor
½ teaspoon sea salt
1 egg

1 bunch of rhubarb, ends trimmed
raw sugar, to sprinkle

For the Pistachio Frangipane, beat the butter, sugar, zests and vanilla for 2–3 minutes until pale.

Add the pistachios and salt and beat briefly to combine.

Add in the egg and beat for about 1–2 minutes. The frangipane will be looking nice and thick and gorgeously green.

Spread the frangipane evenly over the base of the tart. Cut the rhubarb into batons so they fit snugly across the width of the tart and gently press then into the frangipane. You want them nice and tightly packed. When I'm feeling really nerdy (a mood that strikes often) I will arrange them in shades from dark to light; I'm very partial to a bit of fruit ombre!

Sprinkle with raw sugar and bake for 30–35 minutes until the filling feels firm to the touch. Cool completely in the tin before transferring to a serving platter.

Polish Poppyseed Scrolls

Poppyseeds are often seen in Eastern European baking, and these scrolls, or makoviec, are found in every bakery, especially around the Christmas season.

These are truly delicious, not too sweet, and the perfect accompaniment with a mid-morning tea or coffee. If left to my own devices, a batch barely lasts a hot minute at my house.

The poppyseeds don't have to be ground super fine; a rough blitz in a spice grinder will do the job. If you are after a little more texture, sprinkle a handful of chopped walnuts or almonds over the poppyseed filling before rolling.

For the Sour Cream Pastry, in the bowl of a food processor, pulse the flour, icing sugar, butter and yeast until it's the consistency of fine breadcrumbs. Add all remaining ingredients and pulse until the mixture starts forming into clumps. Tip out into a large bowl and bring together with your hands. The dough will be on the firmer side; give it a good 2–3 minutes of elbow grease. Shape into a rectangle, about 2 cm thick. Cover with cling film and let rest for 1 hour at room temperature.

For the filling, combine all the ingredients in a medium pot over a medium heat and cook for 4–5 minutes, stirring often, until the mixture is nice and thick. Set aside to cool completely before using.

When you are ready to start assembling, place the dough on a lightly floured bench and divide in half. Working with one piece at a time, roll the dough out until you have a 20 cm x 30 cm (8 in x 12 in) rectangle, about 5–6 mm (¼ in) in thickness. I use a ruler here to get a perfect rectangle. Keep any pastry trimmings you have; you never know when they could come in handy!

Grease and line a large oven tray. Evenly spread half the poppyseed filling over the dough, leaving a 1 cm (½ in) border all the way around. With the longest end closest to you, roll the dough up into a tight cylinder, with the seam at the bottom. Place on the prepared baking tray and repeat this process with the remaining dough and filling. Lightly cover with a tea towel and set aside to rest for 1 hour.

Preheat the oven to 170°C (325°F) fan-bake. Brush the rolls with egg wash and bake for 35–40 minutes; the rolls should look puffy and golden. Remove from the oven and let cool for 15 minutes. Use a serrated knife to slice the rolls into 2.5 cm (1 in) thick slices.

Arrange the slices on the baking trays, sprinkle with raw sugar and bake for a further 10 minutes. Remove from the oven and allow to cool on the trays.

Serve warm or at room temperature, they're delicious either way!

Sour Cream Pastry

600 g (1 lb 5 oz) plain flour
60 g (2¼ oz) icing sugar
250 g (9 oz) butter
10 g (¼ oz) instant dried yeast
zest of 1 lemon
zest of 1 orange
100 g (3½ oz) sour cream
90 ml (3 fl oz) milk
1 egg yolk

Poppyseed Filling

180 g (6¼ oz) poppyseeds, ground to a rough powder
160 ml (5¼ fl oz) milk
100 g (3½ oz) caster sugar
100 g (3½ oz) dates, pitted and finely chopped
2 teaspoons ground cinnamon
½ teaspoon ground cardamom
¼ tsp flaky salt
zest of 1 lemon
zest of 1 orange

1 egg, beaten for egg wash
30 g (1 oz) raw sugar, to sprinkle

Dough

Chocolate and Orange Babka Buns

Makes 8 buns

It's safe to say I am the babka's biggest fan. There is just something so therapeutic about it — both the making and the eating part! It's the perfect hybrid of bread and cake and once you try it, I'm convinced you will be just as obsessed as I am.

Babka originated in the Jewish communities of Poland, Russia and Ukraine, and can also be found in every bakery in Israel. Initially, it was a way to use up left over Challah dough and traditionally was made with jams, nuts or dried fruit. The dough itself is very similar to a brioche; enriched with butter and eggs. It's just divine.

This recipe uses a dark chocolate-and-orange-scented filling and honestly, it's heavenly. The twisting and forming of the buns is the trickiest part and takes a little practice at first but it's well worth it; the result is rather special and sure to impress — enjoy that smug feeling!

For the dough, place all ingredients, except the butter, in the bowl of a stand mixer with the dough hook attachment at the ready.

Mix on a medium-low speed until a shaggy dough forms. Much like making a standard brioche, add the butter in two lots, allowing it to fully incorporate before adding more. Mix until the dough is glossy, elastic and pulling away from the side of the bowl. Transfer the dough into a greased bowl, cover with cling film and set aside to prove in a warm space until doubled in size; 1–1½ hours.

While the dough is proving, make the filling.

Melt the chocolate and butter together in a small pot over a low heat, stirring constantly so it doesn't catch at the bottom. Once melted, set aside to cool for a minute or two before adding the remaining ingredients. Stir until smooth and completely combined and then set aside to firm up to a spreadable consistency.

Once the dough has doubled in size, remove it from the bowl, place on a lightly floured bench, and cut into 8 even pieces.

Grease and line a large baking tray.

Working with one piece at a time, roll the dough into a rectangle measuring roughly 16 cm (6¼ in) in length, 14 cm (5½ in) in width and 5 mm (¼ in) thick. You want the longest edge closest to you.

Spread about 1 tablespoon of the filling over the dough using a palette knife, leaving a 1 cm (½ in) border free from filling all around.

Dough
530 g (1 lb 2¾ oz) plain flour
100 g (3½ oz) caster sugar
14 g (½ oz) instant dried yeast
3 eggs
120 ml (4 fl oz) lukewarm water
½ teaspoon flaky salt
zest of 1 orange
1 teaspoon vanilla paste
150 g (5½ oz) butter, softened

Chocolate and Orange Filling
60 g (2¼ oz) dark chocolate, roughly chopped
60 g (2¼ oz) butter
35 g (1¼ oz) cocoa
35 g (1¼ oz) icing sugar
1 teaspoon ground cardamom
zest of 1 orange
½ teaspoon sea salt

Orange Syrup
100 g (3½ oz) caster sugar
zest and juice of 1 orange
100 ml (3½ fl oz) water

30 g (1 oz) roasted hazelnuts, to garnish (optional)

Starting with the longest edge closest to you, roll up the dough into a tight cylinder with the seam at the bottom.

Turn the dough 90 degrees, so that the short end is closest to you and using a sharp knife, or pizza cutter, slice lengthways down through the middle of the dough, so you have two long even pieces.

With the cut sides facing upwards, gently press the top end of each half together to seal, then lift the right piece over the left, left over right, until you reach the end; you are essentially making a two-stranded plait. Gently twist the braid into a circle, crossing one end over the other and tucking one end under the bun, and the other through the centre of the bun. Pinch the ends together on the underside of the babka. Place onto the prepared baking tray and repeat with remaining pieces of dough.

Once you have formed all the babkas, cover with cling film and allow to prove for 30 minutes while you make the syrup.

Combine all the ingredients in a small pot over a medium heat, stirring until the sugar has dissolved. Boil for 3–4 minutes until the mixture has thickened slightly. Remove from the heat and set aside to cool.

Preheat the oven to 160°C (315°F) fan-bake.

Bake the babka for 15–20 minutes, loosely covering them with tin foil if they are browning too quickly.

Once cooked, remove from the oven and brush the babkas generously with the orange syrup and allow to cool ever so slightly. Garnish them with hazelnuts, if desired.

Fresh from the oven and warm is exactly how they should be eaten!

Chocolate and Orange Babka Buns

Tahini and Honey Babka Loaf

Tahini and Honey Babka Loaf

I'm in love with this flavour combination. The loaf is a little less labour intensive than the individual twists (see page 102), but just as delicious.

Try to find the best quality tahini you can and always use hulled, as unhulled tahini can be a little on the bitter side.

For the dough, place all ingredients, except the butter, in the bowl of a stand mixer with the dough hook attachment at the ready. Mix on a medium-low speed until a shaggy dough forms. Much like making a standard brioche, add the butter in two lots, allowing it to fully incorporate before adding more.

Mix until the dough is glossy, elastic and pulling away from the side of the bowl. If it is looking especially sticky, add ¼ cup of flour while the mixer is still running. Transfer the dough into a greased bowl, cover with cling film and let prove in a warm space until doubled in size; 1–1½ hours.

While the dough is proving make the filling.

Combine the butter, tahini, honey, salt and vanilla in a small pot and place over a medium heat. Stir until the butter has melted and all the ingredients are incorporated; you want a nice silky smooth consistency. Take off the heat and stir in the icing sugar and water, mixing well. Scrape into a small bowl and refrigerate until you are ready to use; it needs to be nice and spreadable.

Grease and line a deep 30 cm x 15 cm (12 in x 6 in) loaf tin.

Once the dough has doubled, remove it from the bowl and place on a large piece of lightly floured baking paper. Roll out until you have a rectangle roughly 45 cm (17¾ in) long and 30 cm (12 in) wide and spread the filling evenly over the entire surface using a palette knife. With the longest side of dough closest to you, use the baking paper to roll the dough into a tight cylinder. Slide onto a large baking tray and refrigerate for 20–25 minutes. This makes cutting the babka a far easier and neater job.

While the babka is firming up in the fridge, make the syrup.

Combine all the ingredients in a small pot over a medium heat, stirring until the sugar has dissolved. Simmer for 4–5 minutes until thickened slightly before setting aside to cool.

Dough
550 g (1 lb 4 oz) plain flour
100 g (3½ oz) caster sugar
14 g (½ oz) instant dried yeast
3 eggs
120 ml (4 fl oz) lukewarm water
½ teaspoon flaky salt
20 g (¾ oz) white sesame seeds, toasted, plus extra for sprinkling
1 teaspoon vanilla paste
150 g (5½ oz) butter, softened

Tahini and Honey Filling
85 g (3 oz) butter, softened
110 g (3¾ oz) hulled tahini
100 g (3½ oz) honey
1 teaspoon flaky salt
1 teaspoon vanilla paste
140 g (5 oz) icing sugar
2 tablespoons water

Sesame Seed Syrup
80 g (2¾ oz) caster sugar
80 ml (2½ fl oz) water
2 tablespoons sesame seeds, toasted, plus extra for garnish

Remove the dough from the fridge and, with the short end closest to you, slice lengthways down through the middle of the dough, so you have two long, even pieces.

With the cut sides facing upwards, gently press the top end of each half together to seal, then lift the right piece over the left, left over right, until you reach the end. Tuck the ends underneath and gently lift into the prepared loaf tin. Cover and allow to prove for 30 minutes.

Preheat the oven to 160°C (315°F) fan-bake.

Bake the babka for 40–45 minutes, until golden brown, covering with tin foil if it is browning too quickly.

As soon as it emerges from the oven, brush generously with the syrup and sprinkle with extra sesame seeds. Allow to cool in the tin for 10 minutes before slicing into thick slabs and devouring.

Brioche

Bread . . . but better. Soft, light, rich, can be sweet or savoury. These days it seems to be all about the sourdough but brioche will forever be my number-one loaf.

This recipe is so straightforward, I often feel like I should have worked harder to produce such a delicious end result. The real keys to success here are temperatures and a trusty electric mixer. Room-temperature ingredients will aid in the activation of the yeast; the butter absolutely must be soft and squishy but in no way, shape or form melted.

With other doughs, you can often do the whole thing by hand (which always makes me feel rather virtuous) but here, It's helpful to call in the heavy machinery.

Below is the classic, but you'll find other recipes in this book that take this dough in a sweet as well as savoury direction. Please travel both roads, it's worth it.

160 ml (5¼ fl oz) milk
1½ teaspoons instant
  dried yeast
5 egg yolks
375 g (13 oz) plain flour
30 g (1 oz) caster sugar,
  plus extra for dusting
¼ teaspoon sea salt
150 g (5½ oz) butter
1 egg, beaten for egg wash
sugar, to sprinkle

In a small pot, gently heat the milk until lukewarm. Place the yeast in a small bowl and pour over half the warmed milk, stirring to combine. Leave for 8–10 minutes until frothy.

In a separate bowl, mix the remaining milk with the egg yolks and whisk to combine.

In the bowl of a stand mixer, combine the flour, sugar and salt. Make a well in the centre and pour in the yeast and yolk mixtures. Attach the dough hook and mix for about 3–4 minutes until a shaggy dough starts to form. Working slowly now, add the butter, one-third at a time, waiting until each addition has been fully incorporated before adding more. When all the butter has been incorporated, the dough will be looking glossy, shiny and elastic.

Remove the bowl from the mixer, cover with cling film and leave in a warm place until doubled in size.

Preheat the oven to 180°C (350°F) fan-bake. Grease and line a 24 cm (9½ in) loaf tin.

Gently knock back the dough and knead on a lightly floured surface. Shape into a loaf and then transfer to the prepared tin. Cover, and prove once more until doubled in size. Brush the dough with egg wash and sprinkle with sugar. Bake for 25–30 minutes until gorgeously golden and risen. Carefully remove the loaf from the tin and place onto a lined oven tray. Bake for a further 8 minutes until the sides have coloured up nicely.

Allow to cool momentarily on a wire rack, but tuck in while it's still warm; fresh bread drenched in butter is one of life's simple pleasures.

Challah

I have so many fond memories of eating challah. I went to a small Jewish primary school and every Friday we had the opportunity to buy a couple of loaves to take home to our families for Shabbat.

We never really celebrated Shabbat in our household, but we definitely celebrated bread, so every Friday without failure I would hop on the bus home with two pillowy loaves in hand. I don't think the loaves ever survived the 10-minute bus journey intact.

It's almost brioche-like in sweetness, but has this gorgeous thready, pull-apart texture that makes it near impossible to resist. Once you start, it's very hard to stop, so either don't even try it, or commit to the whole loaf! I would choose the latter.

The recipe below is enough for two braids and is best eaten on the day it is made. If there are leftovers however, it's divine lightly toasted with lashings of butter, or turned into French toast.

In a small bowl, combine the water and yeast and 1 teaspoon of the sugar, stirring briefly. Allow to sit for 5–10 minutes until foaming.

In the bowl of a stand mixer, add the eggs, oil, the yeast mixture and the remaining sugar. Mix until combined. With the dough hook attachment ready to go, start mixing on a low speed while you gradually add the flour and salt. Mix for 6–8 minutes until smooth and elastic; the dough may feel slightly firmer than what you may be used to.

Shape into a ball and place in an oiled bowl, cover and allow to rise for 1–2 hours or until doubled in size.

Turn the dough out onto a lightly floured surface and dived into 6 equal balls; I sometimes weigh these out if I'm feeling pedantic.

Cover again and let rise for 10 minutes. Grease and line a large oven tray. Now we are ready to braid. Take three pieces of the dough, roll each piece out into a 40 cm (16 in) long strand and position them side by side on the prepared baking tray. Pinch the tops of the ropes together and braid, pinching them together at the bottom. Tuck the ends under on each side. Repeat this process with the remaining dough, and place on your prepared tray before covering loosely with cling film and allowing to rise for 15 minutes.

Preheat the oven to 170°C (325°F) fan-bake.

Brush each loaf all over with egg wash and sprinkle generously with poppyseeds and flaky salt.

Bake for about 35–40 minutes or until the loaves are a deep brown colour and hollow sounding when tapped. Set aside to cool momentarily before tearing and sharing.

250 ml (9 fl oz/1 cup) lukewarm water
15 g (½ oz) instant dried yeast
50 g (1¾ oz) caster sugar
2 eggs
65 ml (2 fl oz) rapeseed oil
670 g (1 lb 7½ oz) plain flour
¾ tablespoon table salt

To garnish
1 egg, beaten for egg wash
poppyseeds, to garnish
flaky salt

Schnecken

This German-style sweet bun kicks the proverbial out of the standard cinnamon scrolls that saturate most bakeries these days. It's gooier, stickier, fluffier and just far superior in my opinion — give me caramel over gluggy white icing any day.

I've chosen pecans here, but walnuts or almonds work just as well.

Grease and line a 30 cm x 22 cm (12 in x 8½ in) baking dish.

To make the dough, melt the butter in a small pot over a medium-low heat. Add the milk and sugar and heat until lukewarm, stirring to dissolve the sugar. Pour the warm milk mixture into the bowl of the stand mixer and stir in the yeast. Allow the mixture to sit for 10 minutes.

Whisk the whole egg and egg yolk together and add to the yeast mixture, along with the vanilla and salt. Attach the dough hook and with the mixer on a low speed, add the flour in 3 lots, and mix for about 5 minutes, until you have a nice smooth dough. Transfer the dough into a large greased bowl, cover with cling film and allow to prove for 2 hours or until tripled in volume.

For the Brown Sugar Pecan Topping, melt the butter, sugar and liquid glucose in a small pot over a medium-low heat, stirring to combine. Remove from the heat and spread the mixture in the bottom of the prepared dish. Sprinkle with the chopped pecans.

Punch down the dough and turn it out onto a lightly floured bench. Knead for a minute, then use a lightly floured rolling pin to roll the dough into a rectangle about 45 cm (18 in) long and 30 cm (12 in) wide.

Now to fill the schnecken. Brush the dough all over with the butter. In a small bowl, mix together the sugar, spices and salt. Sprinkle the sugar mixture evenly over the melted butter. Starting with the longest edge, roll the dough up into a tight cylinder.

Slice the roll into nine 5 cm (2 in) thick slices and arrange, cut side up, in the prepared baking dish. Cover the baking dish with a tea towel and allow it to rise once more for about 40 minutes.

Preheat the oven to 170°C (325°F) fan-bake.

Bake the schnecken for about 35–40 minutes until golden brown, rotating the pan halfway through the baking time. Check them occasionally during the cook, and if they seem to be browning too quickly, loosely cover them with a sheet of tin foil.

Remove the pan from the oven and cool on a wire rack for 5–10 minutes. Turn the schnecken out of the pan while still warm by inverting the pan over a large platter or baking sheet. Be careful as there will be a fair amount of hot caramel happening. Serve the schnecken warm.

Dough
120 g (4¼ oz) butter, softened
245 g (9 oz) milk
65 g (2½ oz) caster sugar
4 g (⅛ oz) instant dried yeast
1 large egg
1 large egg yolk
1 teaspoon vanilla paste
1½ teaspoons flaky salt
440 g (15½ oz) plain flour

Brown Sugar Pecan Topping
170 g (6 oz) butter
130 g (4¾ oz) brown sugar
85 ml (2¾ fl oz) liquid glucose
100 g (3½ oz) pecans, roughly chopped

Cinnamon Sugar Filling
60 g (2¼ oz) butter, melted and cooled
150 g (5½ oz) brown sugar
1 tablespoon ground cinnamon
1 teaspoon ground ginger
½ teaspoon flaky salt

Fig and Almond Bostock Buns

This is a loose take on the French 'bostock', typically, thick slices of brioche that have been soaked in syrup, topped with frangipane, and baked until crisped.

These buns make for a gorgeous breakfast or afternoon tea. If you want to indulge at breakfast but can't face an early rise, cover the buns once shaped and nestled in the baking dish, and let prove in the fridge overnight. Remove from the fridge 30 minutes before baking.

In a small bowl, combine the figs and orange juice and zest. Give it a mix and set aside.

For the dough, combine all the ingredients in the bowl of a stand mixer with the dough hook attachment. Knead for 10 minutes on a medium-low speed until it is shiny, smooth and elastic. Shape the dough into a ball and transfer to a greased bowl. Cover and allow to prove for 1–1½ hours or until doubled in size.

Meanwhile, get onto the Almond Frangipane.

Beat the butter, sugar, zest, salt and vanilla until fluffy and pale; 2–3 minutes. Add the egg and mix until combined, scraping down the sides to make sure everything is incorporated. Add the ground almonds and beat for 2–3 minutes until thick and aerated.

Grease and line a 22 cm (8½ in) square baking dish.

When the dough has doubled in size, tip it onto a lightly floured bench and roll out to a large rectangle measuring 45 cm x 30 cm (18 in x 12 in).

Spread the frangipane evenly over the dough using a palette knife leaving a 2 cm (¾ in) border. Sprinkle over the figs.

Starting with the longest edge, roll the pastry up into a cylinder. Trim 2 cm (¾ in) off the ends and then cut into 9 even pieces; about 4 cm (1½ in) wide. The dough should slice rather neatly as it's a little on the firmer side, which makes things nice and easy.

Arrange the buns snugly in the prepared baking dish, cover and let prove for 30 minutes.

Preheat the oven to 180°C (350°F) fan-bake.

Bake for 25–30 minutes until beautifully browned. If they are colouring too quickly, cover loosely with tin foil.

As soon as they come out of the oven, brush with the marmalade and allow to cool briefly before diving in.

260 g (9¼ oz) figs, finely chopped
zest and juice of 1 orange

Dough
500 g (1 lb 2 oz) plain flour
75 g (2¾ oz) caster sugar
8 g (¼ oz) instant dried yeast
1 teaspoon vanilla paste
½ teaspoon flaky salt
200 ml (7 fl oz) milk, warmed
100 g (3½ oz) butter, melted and cooled
1 egg

Almond Frangipane
60 g (2¼ oz) butter, softened
75 g (2¾ oz) caster sugar
zest of 1 orange
¼ teaspoon flaky salt
½ teaspoon vanilla paste
1 egg
150 g (5½ oz) ground almonds

For brushing
3 tablespoons marmalade

Good Morning Buns

It's all in the name really. Eat these for breakfast, and you are off to a very good start. These buns always make me think of cinnamon sugar doughnuts but they are slightly more acceptable for the first meal of the day. These buns are best eaten on the day of making, however if there are leftovers, they are divine gently heated and drowned in cream or custard.

For the dough, combine the milk, yeast and 1 teaspoon of the sugar in a small bowl. Mix briefly and allow to sit for 5 minutes or until foamy.

Place all the other ingredients in the bowl of a stand mixer with the dough hook attached. Pour in the milk mixture and mix on medium-low speed for 6–8 minutes until the dough is smooth and elastic.

Transfer to an oiled bowl, cover and allow to prove for 1–1½ hours, or until doubled in size.

Knock the dough back, cover again and rest for a further 10 minutes.

Meanwhile, make the Spiced Sugar Filling. Combine all the ingredients in the bowl of a stand mixer and beat until nice and fluffy; about 2–3 minutes.

Grease a 12-hole standard-sized muffin pan and line the bottom of each hole with a strip of baking paper.

Tip the dough out onto a generously floured benchtop; err on the side of more flour here as it can get very messy if the dough starts to stick.

Roll out to a large rectangle, measuring roughly 45 cm x 32 cm (18 in x 12¾ in) and about 5 mm (¼ in) thick. Using a palette knife, spread the filling over the entire surface and, working quickly and confidently, fold the dough in half lengthways so the filling is all encased and the long seam is closest to you.

Dust the top of the dough in a little extra flour if needed, and then gently roll out to a slightly bigger rectangle, measuring 50 cm x 25 cm (20 in x 10 in).

Using a long, very sharp knife, cut the dough into approximately 4 cm (1½ in) wide strips so you are left with 12 strips. Working with one strip at a time, cut into three even strands, leaving the top 1 cm (½ in) attached. Plait together, and then roll the dough onto itself, into a neat ball; they will look like little braided buns. You want to work relatively quickly here as the warmer the dough and buttery filling gets, the trickier this process can be. Gently tuck into the prepared tin and repeat with the remaining dough. Once they are all braided and rolled, cover the buns, and allow to prove for 30 minutes.

Dough
200 ml milk, lukewarm
12 g instant dried yeast
50 g caster sugar
600 g plain flour
2 eggs
1 tsp flaky salt
200 g butter, softened
1 tsp vanilla paste

Spiced Sugar Filling
150 g (5½ oz) butter, softened
250 g (9 oz) brown sugar
2 teaspoons ground cinnamon
1 tablespoon ground cardamom
½ teaspoon flaky salt
½ teaspoon vanilla paste

60 ml (2 fl oz/¼ cup) milk, for brushing

Cinnamon Sugar
120 g (4¼ oz) caster sugar
½ tablespoon ground cinnamon
1 teaspoon ground cardamom

Preheat the oven to 180°C (350°F) fan-bake.

Brush lightly with milk and bake for 20–25 minutes until golden brown and puffed.

For the Cinnamon Sugar, combine the sugar and spices in a small bowl.

As soon as the buns are ready, remove from the oven and carefully, dunk each one into the bowl of spiced sugar, tossing to coat.

Transfer to a wire rack to cool briefly before enjoying a very good morning.

Raspberry and Pistachio Quark Twists

Nothing pleases me more than a sweet breakfast and these make for the perfect start to the day. The yoghurt in the dough gives it the most gorgeous texture, with a very pleasing amount of chew.

Quark is a soft set cheese, hailing originally from Germany and is seen in a fair amount of Eastern European cooking. It's a bit of a mix between Greek yoghurt and cottage cheese, but with a silky-smooth texture and mild taste.

If you can't track it down, labneh or ricotta are great substitutes.

For the dough, place the flour, yeast, sugar, vanilla, salt and zests into the bowl of a stand mixer with the dough hook attachment at the ready.

Mix the yoghurt and water together in a small jug. Turn the mixer on low and slowly pour in the yoghurt mixture. Mix for 2–3 minutes, until the dough is smooth, turn the mixer off and let rest for 8 minutes.

Mix again for 2 minutes, before covering and allowing to prove for 1 hour or until doubled in size.

For the filling, in a small bowl, combine the raspberries, sugar and pistachios and toss to combine.

Grease and line two large oven trays.

Lightly dust the bench with flour and roll out the dough into a rectangle measuring roughly 45 cm x 30 cm (18 in x 12 in). You want the dough to be about 5 mm (¼ in) thick. Using a palette knife, spread the horizontal middle third of the dough with half of the quark.

Scatter half of the sugar over the quark and top with half of the raspberry mixture. Fold the bottom half of the dough over the raspberries and then spread the remaining quark on top, followed by the remaining brown sugar and raspberry mixture. Fold the top third of the dough down so all the filling is enclosed.

Gently roll with a rolling pin so the layers are sealed before using a very sharp knife to cut into 3 cm (1¼ in) strips. If the dough is very soft chill it in the fridge for 30 minutes to make it easier to cut.

Working with one strip at a time, twist each end in opposite directions and then place on the prepared trays, spaced 4 cm (1½ in) apart to allow for rising. Cover with a clean tea towel and let rest for 15 minutes or until they have puffed slightly.

Preheat the oven to 180°C (350°F) fan-bake. Bake for 20–25 minutes until golden brown. Cool momentarily on the baking trays before transferring to a wire rack. Dust with icing sugar before serving.

Dough
560 g (1 lb 4¼ oz) plain flour
4 g (⅛ oz) instant dried yeast
50 g (1¾ oz) caster sugar
1 teaspoon vanilla paste
1 teaspoon flaky salt
zest of 1 lemon
zest of 1 orange
70 g (2½ oz) Greek yoghurt
220 ml (7¾ fl oz) warm water

Raspberry and Pistachio Quark Filling
180 g (6¼ oz) raspberries
80 g (2¾ oz) caster sugar
60 g (2¼ oz) pistachios, roughly chopped
220 g (7¾ oz) quark
70 g (2½ oz) brown sugar
icing sugar, to dust

Cookies
and Slices

Brown Butter Double Chocolate Cookies

I feel like every man and their dog claims to be in possession of the best chocolate chip cookie recipe. Well, I'm joining the club because these really ARE the best.

Brown butter is the MVP here, giving a gorgeous rich and decadent flavour, but a really important step that shouldn't be ignored is chilling the dough overnight, or if you can, for 48 hours.

Chilling the dough does a few things. For starters, it stops the cookies from spreading too quickly once they go in the oven as the fats are cold and therefore the cookies will expand more slowly and hold their texture better. Nothing is more disappointing than a sad flat disc of a biscuit.

Popping the dough in the fridge also enhances the flavour hugely as the dry ingredients soak up moisture from the wet ingredients. This subtle hydration concentrates the flavours. Post fridge time, the cookies will bake more evenly, look and taste better. Patience really is a virtue.

240 g (8½ oz) butter, roughly chopped
120 g (4¼ oz) caster sugar
270 g (9½ oz) brown sugar
2 teaspoons vanilla paste
2 eggs
325 g (11½ oz) plain flour
1 tablespoon flaky salt, plus extra to sprinkle
½ teaspoon baking soda
225 g (8 oz) milk chocolate, roughly chopped
225 g (8 oz) dark chocolate, roughly chopped

First things first, make your brown butter. Place the butter into a medium pot set over a medium heat. Whisk frequently as it melts. Continue to cook, running the whisk over the bottom of the pan every now and again to loosen up the milk solids. You will see the butter start to foam and then subside, giving way to lightly browned specks. The smell is absolutely heavenly; nutty, toasty and just divine. Don't be too scared to push it here; you want those milk solids seriously toasted. As soon as you reach this point pour the butter into a heatproof bowl to stop it from cooking further, making sure you don't leave behind any of those toasty milk solids; this is liquid gold you're dealing with!

Place your brown butter into the fridge to firm up, we want it softened, but definitely not melted.

Grease and line two large oven trays.

In the bowl of a stand mixer, beat the brown butter, sugars and vanilla for 2–3 minutes until pale and very thick.

Add the eggs one by one, scraping down the side of the bowl in between each addition.

Combine the dry ingredients and sieve over the bowl before mixing briefly until just combined.

Working by hand now, fold in the chopped chocolates.

Weigh out 70 g (2½ oz) balls of cookie dough and place on the prepared trays 3 cm (1¼ in) apart. You should get about 18 cookies; if you gorge yourself on the raw dough like me, you will obviously get fewer! Flatten the cookies ever so slightly with heel of your hand and top with an extra sprinkle of flaky salt.

Cover with cling film and refrigerate for as long as you can cope!

Preheat the oven to 170°C (325°F) fan-bake.

Bake for 12–14 minutes. Allow to cool for 5 minutes on the baking trays before transferring to a wire rack to cool fully.

Brown Butter Double Chocolate Cookies

Tahini Shortbread with Salted Chocolate Ganache

Tahini Shortbread with Salted Chocolate Ganache

Hi, I'm Petra and I am a tahini addict.

I go through at least one jar a week at home and I think it really is an unsung hero in food world — you will see it a few times in this book!

It's like peanut butter's more sophisticated cousin and it works so beautifully in a sweet application, especially when paired with chocolate.

These biscuits are deeply moreish and give the classic shortbread a much-needed makeover.

Always use the hulled tahini, as unhulled can be a little on the bitter side.

Preheat the oven to 180°C (350°F) fan-bake. Line three large trays with baking paper. In the bowl of a stand mixer, beat the butter, sugars and vanilla until super light and fluffy.

Add the tahini and mix again, scraping down the sides to ensure everything is incorporated.

Working by hand now, add the flour and salt and gently fold together until just combined.

Tip the mixture out onto a lightly floured surface and bring together into a dough. It may look a little dry at first but keep working it and it will come together into a soft dough.

Roll out into a rectangle about 5 mm (¼ in) thick and punch out cookies using a 5 cm (2 in) round cookie cutter. Place on the trays, allowing 2 cm (¾ in) between each biscuit to allow for spreading. It is a pretty resilient dough, so you can re-work and re-roll as many times as needed.

Brush each biscuit with egg white and generously sprinkle with sesame seeds.

Bake for 10–12 minutes until lightly brown.

Allow to cool completely on the baking trays.

While the cookies are cooling, get onto the Salted Chocolate Ganache.

Combine the cream, tahini and salt in a small pot and bring to a simmer over a medium heat, stirring continuously so the cream does not burn.

Tahini Shortbread

200 g (7 oz) unsalted butter, softened

90 g (3½ oz) caster sugar

90 g (3¼ oz) light brown sugar

1 teaspoon vanilla paste

110 g (5½ oz) hulled tahini

385 g (13¾ oz) plain flour

¾ teaspoon salt

1 large egg white

black and white sesame seeds

Salted Chocolate Ganache

150 ml (5 fl oz) cream

45 g (1¾ oz) tahini

1 teaspoon flaky salt

150 g (5½ oz) dark chocolate, chopped

Place the chocolate in a heatproof bowl and pour over the hot cream mixture. Let it sit for a couple of minutes before stirring until smooth and glossy.

Set aside to thicken up until it is a spreadable consistency, before transferring to a piping bag.

Pipe generous (and I mean generous) dollops of the ganache onto half the cookies before sandwiching together with the second cookie.

The cookies will keep in the fridge for a good 4–5 days.

Miso and Roasted White Chocolate Cookies

What a combo! Two of my favourite flavours combined into one hell of a treat. White chocolate gets such a bad rap and you know what, it kind of deserves it. It's just too sweet, cloyingly sweet in fact. And it's not even chocolate! I don't know about you, but it's always made me feel cheated.

The roasting process is such a good trick as it turns this sickly situation into a roasty, toasty, caramel-noted dream and makes the absolute world of difference. You will literally never NOT roast white chocolate again after you have tried this.

In terms of the miso, try and find white miso if you can. It's slightly milder than the other varieties with a gorgeous mellow, nutty sweetness.

280 g (10 oz) white chocolate buttons
220 g (7¾ oz) butter, softened
200 g (7 oz) brown sugar
150 g (5½ oz) caster sugar
2 teaspoons vanilla paste
100 g (3½ oz) white miso
½ teaspoon flaky salt
2 eggs
415 g (14¾ oz) plain flour
1 teaspoon baking soda
100 g (3½ oz) white sesame seeds, lightly toasted

Preheat the oven to 160°C (315°F) fan-bake. Grease and line 2 large oven trays.

First things first, roast the white chocolate. Place the buttons on one of the prepared trays, spread out into a single layer, and roast for 10–12 minutes until nice and golden. Set aside to cool, before roughly chopping.

In a large bowl, beat the butter, sugars, vanilla, miso and salt until pale and thick; about 2–3 minutes.

Add the eggs one by one, beating well after each addition.

Sieve over the flour and baking soda and beat again briefly until just incorporated.

Working by hand now, fold through the roasted white chocolate.

Chill the dough for 1 hour to firm up. Weigh out 60 g (2¼ oz) balls of cookie dough, roll each one in the toasted sesame seeds so they are completely covered and place on the prepared trays 3 cm (1¼ in) apart. You should get about 24 cookies. Flatten the cookies slightly with the heel of your hand.

Cover with cling film and refrigerate overnight.

Preheat the oven to 170°C (325°F) fan-bake.

Bake the cookies for 14–15 minutes; you want them a little on the softer side.

Allow them to cool on the trays for 10 minutes before transferring them to a wire rack (or your mouth).

Pine Nut Caramel Shortbread

This is caramel slice, all grown up . . . I'm not sure I need to say much more.

If you can track down Pinoli pine nuts, I thoroughly recommend using them. They are grown in Marlborough and are hands down the most gorgeous pine nuts around. They are rich, buttery and make the world of difference in this bake.

Preheat the oven to 185°C (360°F) fan-bake. Grease and line a 23 cm (9 in) square baking tin.

For the Shortbread Base, combine the sugar and butter in a small pot and melt over a medium heat, stirring continuously. Remove from the heat and allow to cool for a couple of minutes before stirring through the remaining ingredients. The mixture should be soft and dough-like in texture.

Spread over the base of the tin and even out with a palette knife.

Bake for 10–12 minutes until golden brown. Remove from the oven and set aside.

For the Pine Nut Caramel, combine the butter, golden syrup, condensed milk and vanilla in a medium pot and place over a medium heat. Stir until the butter has melted and the mixture is smooth. Take the pot off the heat and stir through the salt and pine nuts.

Pour over the top of the base, sprinkle with a little more flaky salt and cook for 15–20 minutes; the caramel will have turned a gorgeous burnished gold in colour.

Allow to cool completely in the tin before cutting in half and slicing into 16 generous fingers.

Shortbread Base
115 g (4 oz) brown sugar
100 g (3½ oz) butter
85 g (3 oz) plain flour
85 g (3 oz) self-raising flour
100 g (3½ oz) ground almonds
¼ teaspoon flaky salt

Pine Nut Caramel
30 g (1 oz) butter, softened
60 g (2¼ oz) golden syrup
400 g (14 oz) condensed milk
1 teaspoon vanilla paste
1 teaspoon flaky salt, plus extra to sprinkle
160 g (5¾ oz) Pinoli pine nuts

Almond Butter Brownie

I have a strong and instant distrust for anyone who does not unequivocally love brownie. It's one of the most nostalgic baked goods, and I think the older I get, the more I appreciate its simplicity.

This one is my tried and true, and always the recipe I call on when I need a treat but am seriously lacking in energy. It is a total cinch to put together; quite literally a one-pot wonder.

It's gluten-free as it's made with ground almonds, which creates the fudgy dense texture that's always the goal in the brownie game. The naughty addition of almond butter swirled through it isn't exactly necessary but 'everything in moderation including excess' is a motto I live by so here we are. Eat while still warm . . . sheer bliss.

Preheat the oven to 170°C (325°F) fan-bake. Grease and line a 25 cm x 30 cm (10 in x 12 in) rectangular tin.

Place the chocolate and butter in a medium pot and stir over a low heat until fully melted. You could of course do this in a bowl over a pot of simmering water, but truth be told, I find bain maries rather cumbersome and I avoid them whenever possible. As long as you stir thoroughly, there will no burning happening here.

Remove from the heat then add the vanilla and sugar straight into the pot while the chocolate and butter is still hot and stir for a few minutes until the sugar starts to dissolve. Let cool for 4–5 minutes.

Whisk the eggs in a small bowl and then pour into the chocolate mix, whisking again until the batter is smooth and shiny.

Fold through the ground almonds and salt, mix gently with a rubber spatula until just combined and then pour into the prepared tin.

Dollop the almond butter in six lots around the brownie and, using a skewer or small knife, swirl it through the chocolate batter. Don't worry about the top being smooth and flat; texture is your friend here.

Bake for 45–50 minutes; there should still be a little gooey give in the centre when pressed.

Allow to cool for as long as you can bear to wait; but please eat it while it's still warm!

450 g (1 lb) dark chocolate (60% cocoa solids), roughly chopped
450 g (1 lb) butter, softened
3 teaspoons vanilla paste
400 g (14 oz) caster sugar
6 eggs
500 g (1 lb 2 oz) ground almonds
1 teaspoon flaky salt
250 g (9 oz) almond butter (I use Fix & Fogg Crunchy, which is divine)

Ginger Kisses

In my opinion, ginger kisses are one of the most iconic biscuits and have always been a firm favourite of mine. I remember absolutely inhaling these by the packet whenever I got the chance. I could never ever, and still can't, stop at one.

This recipe has been tweaked over and over, searching for that unmistakable ginger kiss pillowy texture. I'm embarrassed to admit how much of a headache these caused me; who would have thought that recreating this humble biscuit would be such a schlep! Big thanks to my mum who was my chief taster.

That being said, I'm happy to report . . . I think we've nailed it!

Grease and line three oven trays.

For the Ginger Biscuits, in a large bowl, mix all the dry ingredients together.

In the bowl of a stand mixer, beat the butter, sugar, golden syrup and vanilla for 2–3 minutes until light and fluffy.

Add the eggs one by one, scraping down the side of the bowl after each addition.

With the mixer on a low speed, add the dry ingredients in three batches and mix until fully incorporated; the mixture should be rather dense. Transfer to a piping bag and cut a 2 cm (¾ in) opening.

Pipe the biscuits onto the prepared trays so they are about 4 cm (1¼ in) in diameter, being mindful to space them at least 3 cm (1¼ in) apart. You want to end up with about 50, which I know sounds like a lot but trust me, you can never have too many.

Place the trays in the fridge for 1 hour to firm up.

Preheat the oven to 180°C (350°F) fan-bake.

Sprinkle the chilled biscuits lightly with some extra raw sugar and bake for 10–12 minutes until golden brown. They should have puffed up like cute little pillows.

Using a palette knife or spatula, transfer the biscuits immediately to a wire rack to cool completely.

While they are cooling, get onto the Golden Syrup Buttercream.

In the bowl of a stand mixer, beat the butter, cream cheese, golden syrup, ginger and salt until completely smooth and creamy. Add the icing sugar, one-third of a cup at a time and beat until silky and thick. Transfer to a piping bag and cut a 2 cm (¾ in) opening.

When you are ready to fill the biscuits, pipe a generous dollop on the bottom of half the biscuits before sandwiching them together with their frosting-free mate. The filled cookies are best eaten within 2 days.

Ginger Biscuits
250 g (9 oz) plain flour
170 g (6 oz) self-raising flour
20 g (¾ oz) ground ginger
½ teaspoon baking soda
½ teaspoon flaky salt
150 g (5½ oz) butter, softened
240 g (8½ oz) raw caster sugar, plus extra to sprinkle
80 g (2¾ oz) golden syrup
1 teaspoon vanilla paste
4 eggs

Golden Syrup Buttercream
100 g (3½ oz) butter, softened
200 g (7 oz) cream cheese, softened
85 g (3 oz) golden syrup
10 g (¼ oz) ground ginger
1 teaspoon flaky salt
400 g (14 oz) icing sugar

Greek Honey Syrup Cookies

These are so moreish. So much so, that I would stretch to the word 'addictive'. I'm writing this after making them this morning; the recipe below makes 20, yet for some strange reason I can't put my finger on, I only had 16 when I packed them away. Total mystery really . . .

A bit of a riff on the classic Greek biscuit melomakarona, which are typically served around Christmas, these biscuits are almost a hybrid between a cookie and a cake. A rather sensational union if you ask me.

They keep for up to four days in an airtight container, but I implore you to try one when it is still warm and glistening from its honey-syrup bath. It's pretty special.

Firstly, make the syrup. Combine all the ingredients in a small pot and stir over a medium heat until the sugar has dissolved. Bring to the boil and simmer for 4–5 minutes before removing from the heat and allowing to cool completely.

Grease and line four oven trays.

For the cookies, whisk the oil, icing sugar and brandy in a large bowl. Add the zest and orange juice and whisk to combine.

In a separate bowl, combine all the dry ingredients and mix to combine.

Add the dry ingredients to the oil mixture and, using a rubber spatula, gently mix until fully incorporated.

Weigh out 60 g (2¼ oz) balls of cookie dough and place on the prepared trays 2 cm (¾ in) apart. Gently flatten each cookie with the heel of your hand before chilling in the fridge for 1 hour.

Preheat the oven to 170°C (325°F) fan-bake. Set up a wire rack inside of a large, rimmed baking tray; this is to catch any stray syrup post biscuit soak.

Bake the cookies for 20–25 minutes. They should be golden brown but still slightly soft in the centre.

As soon as they are ready, carefully dunk each hot cookie in the cool syrup. Place on the wire rack and sprinkle generously with the chopped walnuts, pressing gently so they stick.

Allow to cool completely to room temperature . . . or not.

Spiced Honey Syrup
400 g (14 oz) caster sugar
2 cinnamon sticks
5 cloves
2 star anise
120 g (4¼ oz) mānuka honey
300 ml (10½ fl oz) water

Cookies
315 ml (10¾ fl oz) olive oil
30 g (1 oz) icing sugar
2 tablespoons brandy
zest and juice (240 ml (8 fl oz)) of 2 large oranges
1½ teaspoons ground cinnamon
½ teaspoon ground nutmeg
½ teaspoon ground cloves
½ teaspoon flaky salt
500 g (1 lb 2 oz) plain flour
110 g (3¾ oz) semolina
½ teaspoon baking soda

To garnish
120 g (4¼ oz) walnuts, roughly chopped

Baci Di Dama

These gluten-free sandwich cookies hail from Tortona in northern Italy and are total melt-in-your-mouth heaven. They are delicate, buttery and deeply moreish. You can use any kind of chocolate you want to sandwich them together; Nutella also works a treat.

    If you are grinding your own hazelnuts, make sure you roast them first to enhance the flavour. Rub the skins off in between a tea towel as soon as they come out of the oven.

    The dough can be kept in the freezer for about a month, so feel free to double this recipe so you have delicious cookies on hand at the drop of a hat.

140 g (5 oz) ground hazelnuts
140 g (5 oz) rice flour
100 g (3½ oz) butter, softened
100 g (3½ oz) caster sugar
1 teaspoon vanilla paste
55 g (2 oz) milk or dark chocolate

Grease and line two large oven trays.

    Place all ingredients, except the chocolate, in a large bowl and using your fingers, rub the mixture together until it resembles coarse breadcrumbs.

    Keep working the mixture until you form a soft dough; this cookie is pretty resilient so you don't have to worry too much about overworking the dough.

    Weigh out 16 g (½ oz) neat balls of cookie dough and place on the prepared trays, 2 cm (¾ in) apart. We don't want to flatten these down at all. You should end up with 24 balls. Chill in the fridge for 1 hour.

    Preheat the oven to 160°C (315°F) fan-bake

    Bake the cookies for 10 minutes, swap the trays so they colour evenly, then bake for a further 5 minutes.

    Allow to cool completely on the trays.

    Once you are ready to assemble, melt the chocolate in a small pot, stirring continuously so it doesn't catch on the bottom.

    Dollop ½ teaspoon chocolate on the bottom side of one cookie before sandwiching it with another.

    Once all the biscuits are filled and sandwiched, set them sideways on a wire rack until the chocolate is firm and set.

Pistachio Amaretti

Makes 24 biscuits

A twist on the almond-based classic, these biscuits are so tasty and everyone I have ever made them for promptly falls in love with them. The moist fudgy texture in these cookies couldn't be better and the pistachio flavour is so rich and decadent here. They really could rival the almond-only original; a bold claim I know, but I'm making it.

Preheat the oven to 170°C (325°F) fan-bake. Grease and line two large oven trays.

Combine the ground nuts and salt in a large bowl and stir to combine.

In a separate bowl, whisk the egg whites, zest and vanilla until fluffy and thick; about 3–4 minutes.

Sieve the icing sugar over the egg whites and fold to combine. Add in the ground nut mixture and stir until fully incorporated. The mixture should be thick and a little on the sticky side.

Roll the dough into 24 small balls; damp hands are quite helpful here. Roll each cookie in icing sugar and place on the prepared trays 2 cm (¾ in) apart; we want to leave them in balls here, so don't flatten them at all.

Bake for 15–20 minutes. The cookies are done when lightly browned and cracks have formed on the surface.

Allow the biscuits to cool for 5 minutes on the baking trays before transferring to a wire rack to cool completely.

The amaretti will keep for up to 6 days stored in an airtight container at room temperature.

180 g (6¼ oz) pistachios, finely ground in a food processor
300 g (10½ oz) ground almonds
½ teaspoon flaky salt
4 egg whites
zest of 1 orange
½ teaspoon vanilla paste
380 g (13½ oz) icing sugar, plus 100 g (3½ oz) extra for rolling

144

COOKIES AND SLICES

Baklava

All self-control promptly goes out the window when I lay eyes on this syrupy beauty. Every time I make this, I'm always amazed at how something so heavenly can come from such few ingredients.

It's hard to pinpoint the exact origins of baklava, with both Greece and Turkey staking claims. Turkish baklava is almost always filled with pistachio nuts and a plain sugar syrup, whereas traditional Greek baklava is mainly made with walnuts and an aromatic-laced soak. I tend to favour the latter version, but this recipe can easily be adapted, with the walnuts swapped out and aromatics removed.

Start the syrup first. Place all the ingredients in a medium pot and cook over a medium heat, stirring until the sugar has completely dissolved. Bring to a simmer and cook for 10–12 minutes on a low heat until slightly thickened. Remove from the heat and let cool completely.

Preheat the oven to 175°C (335°F) fan-bake. Butter the base and sides of a 22 cm x 30 cm (8½ in x 12 in) baking tin.

Place the walnuts in the bowl of a food processor and pulse until roughly chopped; this can also be done by hand.

Place a sheet of filo in the base of the prepared tin. Brush with butter and top with another sheet of filo. Repeat this process until you have 5 sheets of filo. Sprinkle ½ a cup of the chopped walnuts evenly over the pastry. Repeat this process three more times; we want to end up with 4 layers of walnuts each with a layer of 5 sheets of filo on the top. Make sure you are buttering every sheet liberally with butter. As always, more is more.

Using a sharp knife, cut diagonal slices 4 cm (1¼ in) apart, cutting all the way to the bottom of the pan. Cut again on the opposite side to make little diamonds.

Bake the baklava for 30–40 minutes or until golden and crisped.

Once cooked, remove from the oven and immediately drench with the cooled syrup. Allow to cool completely in the pan before transferring a serving platter and scattering with pistachios and dried rose petals.

Spiced Syrup
550 g (1 lb 4 oz) caster sugar
500 ml (17 fl oz/2 cups) water
skin of 1 lemon
4 whole cloves
1 cinnamon stick

280 g (10 oz) walnuts
25 sheets filo pastry
185 g (6½ oz) butter, melted

To decorate
50 g (1¾ oz) pistachios, roughly chopped
1 tablespoon dried rose petals

Halvah Truffles

The ancient origins of this candy are disputed, with some claiming that India and others that Turkey are responsible for this heavenly thing.

There are hundreds of variations of halvah across the globe but the most common, and my personal favourite, is the flaky, dense tahini-based version.

I remember walking through the Machane Yehuda market in Jerusalem and being totally gobsmacked by the halvah merchants, their tables piled high with sesame bricks, bejewelled with pistachios and dried flowers.

The chocolate coating is by no means necessary, but I must say I struggle to find a time when chocolate is not a good idea.

375 g (13 oz) hulled tahini
1 teaspoon vanilla paste
1 teaspoon ground
  cardamom
½ teaspoon flaky salt
300 g (10½ oz) caster
  sugar
120 ml (4 fl oz) water
250 g (9 oz) milk or dark
  chocolate
70 g (2½ oz) pistachios,
  roughly chopped

Grease and line a 24 cm (9½ in) loaf tin.

In a small pot, gently heat the tahini until it's softened and loosened. You don't want it hot by any means; if the tahini you have is quite runny already you can skip this step.

Pour the tahini into the bowl of a stand mixer with the paddle attachment at the ready, and add the vanilla, cardamom and salt.

Meanwhile, in another small pot, heat the sugar and water over a medium heat, stirring constantly until the sugar has dissolved. Bring to the boil and simmer for 3–4 minutes or until just starting to thicken.

Start beating the tahini mixture on a low speed and slowly stream in the hot sugar syrup. The mixture should start to pull away from the sides of the bowl and be fully combined and shiny. This won't take long at all, and you don't want to over-mix, so as soon as the mixture comes together, stop beating.

Tip the halvah into the prepared loaf tin and press in until even and flat. Cover with cling film and refrigerate overnight.

Line a baking tray with baking paper.

Remove the halvah from the fridge and cut into bite-sized pieces.

In a small pot, melt whatever chocolate you choose to use.

Using two forks, dip each piece of halvah in the chocolate until fully coated. Place on the lined tray and sprinkle with chopped pistachios; make sure you do this while the chocolate is still wet so the nuts stick. Allow to set at room temperature.

The truffles will keep for over a month in an airtight container at room temperature.

Mandelbrot

While it may look like a classic biscotti, I guarantee that Mandelbrot is better. It is double baked but, unlike its Italian counterpart, this ancient Ashkenazi treat is far richer in eggs and fats, resulting in a cookie that is softer and more delicate. Traditionally they are made with olive oil but as expected, I always use butter, which makes for a far more delicious end product.

You can substitute the walnuts with any nut of your preference, and if chocolate doesn't do it for you, currants or dates work beautifully as well.

In a medium bowl, combine all the dry ingredients, mixing well.

Place the butter, sugar, vanilla, almond extract and zests in the bowl of a stand mixer and whisk on a medium speed until combined.

Add the eggs one by one and mix until thick and pale; about 2–3 minutes.

Working by hand now, add in the dry ingredients and gently fold together until just combined. Add the chocolate and walnuts and mix well. Cover the bowl with cling film and refrigerate until firm; about 1–2 hours.

Preheat the oven to 175°C (335°F) fan-bake. Grease and line two large oven trays.

Tip the dough out on a lightly floured surface and divide into two pieces. Shape each piece of dough into logs measuring approximately 33 cm (13 in) long x 5 cm (2 in) wide x 2.5 cm (1 in) high.

Place on the prepared trays and bake for 25 minutes until lightly golden. You may need to swap the trays halfway through baking to ensure they cook evenly.

Remove from the oven and let cool for 10–15 minutes.

Reduce the oven temperature to 130°C (250°F) fan-bake.

In a small bowl, combine the sugar and cinnamon for dusting.

When the dough has cooled, cut them diagonally into 2 cm (¾ in) thick slices; I tend to do this directly on the baking trays with a sharp serrated knife.

Flip the biscuits onto their sides and sprinkle with half the cinnamon sugar. Flip onto the other side and sprinkle with the remaining sugar.

Bake the mandelbrot for 20 minutes, flip over and cook for a further 20 minutes until golden and crisp. Remove from the oven and allow to cool completely on the baking trays; they will crisp up as they cool.

The mandelbrot will keep for up to 2 weeks in an airtight container at room temperature.

390 g (13¾ oz) plain flour
2 teaspoons baking powder
1 teaspoon flaky salt
1¼ teaspoons ground cinnamon
¼ teaspoon ground nutmeg
245 g (9 oz) butter, melted and cooled
200 g (7 oz) caster sugar
2 teaspoons vanilla paste
¼ teaspoon almond extract
zest of 1 lemon
zest of 1 orange
3 eggs
180 g (6¼ oz) dark chocolate, roughly chopped
100 g (3½ oz) walnuts, roasted and roughly chopped

For dusting
30 g (1 oz) caster sugar
¼ teaspoon ground cinnamon

Maamoul — Arabian Date Cookie

Maamoul originated in ancient Egypt and have since been adopted by many places in the Middle East, often being made to celebrate Easter, Eid or, in the Jewish communities, Purim. Traditionally, they are a shortbread-style biscuit, stuffed with date paste and then pressed into intricately carved wooden moulds before baking.

The filling is fragrant with spices and the dough is divinely flavoured with rose water and orange blossom. The combination is rather heavenly. I have turned the traditional biscuits into a slice in this recipe but the flavours of the ancient original still ring true.

To make the dough, in a large bowl, mix all the dry ingredients until combined. Add the butter, rose water, orange blossom water and zest and rub together with your fingertips until the butter is dispersed evenly. Cover and rest at room temperature for 2 hours; we want to allow time for the semolina to soak up all that gorgeous butter.

Meanwhile get onto the filling.

Place the dates and water in the bowl of a food processor and blend until smooth. Tip into a large bowl and add all the remaining ingredients, mixing well to combine.

Preheat the oven to 180°C (350°F) fan-bake. Grease and line a 22 cm (8½ in) square baking tin.

Divide the rested dough into two and roll out each piece to the same size as the prepared tin. If the dough feels a little too crumbly, add 1–2 tablespoons of water to bring it together.

Place one piece of dough in the bottom of the tin, pressing into place, ensuring it is as even as possible.

Spread the date filling over the top using a palette knife and top with the remaining piece of dough. Using a sharp knife, cut diagonal slices 4 cm (1¼ in) apart, cutting all the way to the bottom of the pan. Cut again on the opposite side to make little diamonds.

Bake the maamoul for 40–50 minutes until the top is sandy brown in colour and the edges are golden.

Cool completely in the pan before carefully transferring to a serving platter and dusting with icing sugar.

Dough
340 g (11¾ oz) coarse semolina
160 g (5¾ oz) fine semolina
80 g (2¾ oz) caster sugar
½ teaspoon ground cinnamon
½ teaspoon instant dried yeast
¼ teaspoon flaky salt
210 g (7½ oz) butter, melted and cooled
2 teaspoons rose water
2 teaspoons orange blossom water
zest of ½ lemon

Spiced Date Filling
600 g (1 lb 5 oz) Medjool dates, pitted and chopped
125 ml (4 fl oz/½ cup) warm water
zest of 1 orange
zest of ½ lemon
¼ teaspoon almond extract
1 teaspoon ground cinnamon
½ teaspoon ground cardamom
¼ teaspoon nutmeg
¼ teaspoon flaky salt

icing sugar, to dust

Savoury

Leek and Cheddar Brioche Butter Pudding

This is the most luxurious brunch known to man. The brioche dough is given a subtle tweak with the addition of aged cheddar, whose presence, in my opinion, never does anything but great things.

The pudding will keep in the fridge for up to 4 days. Just fry thick slices off in a little butter and it is brand new again.

For the brioche dough, combine the milk, sugar and yeast in a jug. Mix and let sit for 5 minutes or until foamy.

Place all the remaining ingredients in the bowl of a stand mixer with the dough hook attachment. Add the milk mixture and mix on a medium-low speed for 6–8 minutes until the dough is shiny and smooth. Transfer to an oiled bowl, cover with cling film and let rise for about 1 hour or until doubled in size.

Grease and line a 24 cm (9½ in) loaf tin and a large baking tray.

Knock the dough back before shaping into the loaf tin. Cover again and let prove for 30 minutes.

Preheat the oven to 180°C (350°F) fan-bake.

Bake the brioche for 35–45 minutes or until it is deep golden brown and sounds hollow when tapped. Turn out onto a wire rack and let it cool for 5–10 minutes before cutting it into 2 cm (¾ in) cubes. Spread the cubes of bread in an even layer on the prepared baking tray and bake for a further 5–10 minutes or until golden brown. Remove from the oven and set aside.

Reduce the oven temperature to 150°C (300°F) fan-bake.

For the Leek Filling, melt the butter in a large frypan over a medium heat and sauté the shallot, leeks and garlic for 10–12 minutes until nice and soft. Remove from the heat, stir through the thyme leaves and season to taste.

In a large jug, whisk the crème fraiche, cream, eggs, egg yolks and mustards. Season to taste. Mix both grated cheeses in a small bowl and toss to combine.

Grease and line a 30 cm (12 in) deep loaf tin. Scatter one-third of the grated cheese at the base of the tin followed by half the leek mixture and half the cubed brioche. Repeat with remaining ingredients then pour over the crème fraiche mixture. Allow to sit for 20 minutes so the brioche can start absorbing all that delicious cream before scattering the remaining cheese on top and baking for 1–1¼ hours until golden brown on top and an inserted skewer comes out clean. Cool in the tin for 10 minutes before serving with extra mustard.

Cheddar Brioche

120 ml (4 fl oz) milk, warmed
10 g (¼ oz) caster sugar
14 g (½ oz) instant dried yeast
450 g (1 lb) plain flour
1 teaspoon flaky salt
1 teaspoon freshly cracked black pepper
100 g (3½ oz) butter, softened
80 g (2¾ oz) crème fraiche
80 g (2¾ oz) cheddar, grated
2 eggs

Leek Filling

50 g (1¾ oz) butter
1 shallot, finely chopped
2 large leeks, white part only, thinly sliced
4 cloves garlic, finely chopped
3 sprigs of thyme, leaves picked

To assemble

350 g (12 oz) crème fraiche
500 ml (17 fl oz/2 cups) cream
2 eggs
2 egg yolks
2 teaspoons Dijon mustard
2 teaspoons wholegrain mustard
140 g (5 oz) aged cheddar, grated
140 g (5 oz) parmesan, grated

Leek and Cheddar Brioche Butter Pudding

Pissaladière

My dad used to make this all the time when we were growing up. Whenever he finds a recipe he loves, he will make it multiple times a week until you literally never want to see it again. These little flurries he has with certain recipes are still a running joke in our family; I still can't eat any variation of eggplant parmigiana!

Pissaladière, though, was one of the few recipes that I never got sick of. It's so savoury, salty and satisfying. Don't rush the cooking of the onions. It's a low and slow process but it's absolutely essential to the success of this dish and worth the wait 10 times over.

In a large pot, heat the oil over a low heat and cook the onions, garlic, thyme and oregano for 1 hour, stirring every now and then. You want them to be super tender with minimal colour on them.

Add in the chopped tomatoes and chilli flakes, and cook for another 5–10 minutes until the mixture has thickened. Season to taste, remove from the heat and set aside to cool completely.

To make the dough, combine the flour, salt and butter in the bowl of a stand mixer and rub together with your fingertips until it resembles fine breadcrumbs. Make a well in the centre. Mix the yeast and water until you have a thick paste. Add to the well along with the egg, and, with the dough hook attachment, mix for 10 minutes until smooth and elastic.

Transfer to an oiled bowl, cover, and allow to prove for 1 hour, or until doubled in size.

Preheat the oven to 200°C (400°F) fan-bake. Grease and line a large baking tray and sprinkle over the polenta.

Tip out the dough onto the tray and roll out to a rectangle, about 5 mm (¼ in) thick. Spread the onion mixture evenly over the dough and arrange the anchovies in crosses; 8 in total. Dot with olives.

Cover and let rest for 10 minutes until the dough has puffed slightly, before baking for 15–20 minutes until golden brown and crisped on the bottom.

Pissaladière is divine eaten straight from the oven or at room temperature sprinkled with chopped Italian parsley.

Pissaladière Topping

50 ml (1¾ fl oz) good-quality olive oil

3 large red onions (approx. 500 g/1 lb 2 oz) thinly sliced

3 cloves garlic, finely chopped

1 tablespoon picked thyme leaves

½ teaspoon dried oregano

2 large tomatoes, blanched, peeled, deseeded and roughly chopped

½ teaspoon chilli flakes

16 anchovies

12 Kalamata olives, halved

Dough

150 g (5½ oz) plain flour

1 teaspoon flaky salt

60 g (2¼ oz) butter, cold and diced

14 g (½ oz) instant dried yeast

1 tablespoon water

1 egg

3 tablespoons fine polenta, for dusting

chopped Italian parsley, to serve

Shallot Tarte Tatin

While most of us are familiar with the traditional fruit-based tarte tatin, I am a big advocate of its savoury sister, and this burnished, sticky shallot version is rather beautiful.

Don't be intimidated by making your own puff pastry. The main difference between classic puff and the rough version, is that here we are blitzing up the butter into small pieces as opposed to incorporating one large slab. This rough puff recipe is absolutely foolproof and a total cheat's version that results in buttery flaky pastry requiring far less effort that the traditional. After all, life is just too short to slave away over a huge slab of butter, and that's a big statement coming from someone like me!

If you don't have the right-sized ovenproof frypan, simply transfer the shallots to a small, greased pie dish or shallow cake tin before topping with the pastry.

For the Rough Puff Pastry, combine the flour, salt and butter in the bowl of a food processor. Pulse until the mixture resembles coarse breadcrumbs; we want little chunks of butter.

Tip into a large bowl, make a well in the centre, add the water and bring the dough together with your hands. Shape into a rectangle, about 2 cm (¾ in) thick, wrap in cling film and rest in the fridge for 30 minutes.

Turn the dough out onto a lightly floured bench, and roll until it is three times the width, about 20 cm x 50 cm (8 in x 20 in). Try to keep the edges as straight and even as possible if you can. You may see some streaks of butter; don't overwork these. A little bit of marbling is ideal here.

Fold the top third of the dough down to the centre, and then the bottom third up and over that. Give the dough a quarter turn to the left or right and then roll out again to three times the length. Fold as before, wrap in cling film and chill again for 30 minutes.

Repeat this rolling, folding and chilling process twice more and then the pastry will be ready to use.

For the Caramelised Shallots, in a 25 cm (10 in) ovenproof frypan, melt the butter and 3 tablespoons of the oil over a medium heat. Add the shallots cut side up, making sure you have enough halves to cover the base of the pan. Cook for 3–4 minutes before sprinkling with sugar and carefully flipping over with a palette knife. This is where you need to take a little care in arranging them neatly, so the base is covered with minimal gaps.

Rough Puff Pastry
225 g (8 oz) plain flour
1 teaspoon flaky salt
225 g (8 oz) butter, cold and diced
90 ml (3 fl oz) cold water

Caramelised Shallots
20 g (¾ oz) butter
4 tablespoons olive oil
5–6 banana shallots, peeled and cut in half lengthways
3 tablespoons brown sugar
60 ml (2 fl oz/¼ cup) balsamic vinegar
2 tablespoons brandy
2 sprigs thyme, leaves picked, plus extra to garnish
1 sprig of rosemary, leaves picked
1 teaspoon flaky salt
1 teaspoon freshy crackled black pepper

Reduce the heat to low and add the vinegar and brandy. Add the thyme and rosemary leaves and continue to cook for a further 5 minutes; give the pan a gentle shake every now and then. The shallots should be caramelising up a treat by now.

Sprinkle with salt and pepper and drizzle with the remaining tablespoon of oil.

Preheat the oven to 190°C (375°F) fan-bake

On a lightly floured bench, roll the pastry out to a 28 cm (11¼ in) diameter circle.

Carefully lay the disc of pastry over the top of the pan, tucking the pastry over the shallots, making sure it's nestled right into the edges of the pan. You can do this with the end of the palette knife or a wooden spoon to avoid hot fingertips.

Bake for 25–30 minutes or until the pastry is gorgeously golden. Remove from the oven and allow to sit for 2–3 minutes.

Place a wooden board or plate on top of the pan, making sure it's a fair bit bigger than the frypan itself. Carefully flip the pan and board over to turn out the tarte. You want to be quick and confident here; mind any stray caramel that could seep out.

Serve immediately topped with fresh thyme leaves.

Shallot Tarte Tatin

Za'atar Buns

Za'atar Buns

Many Palestinians have a deep-rooted love affair with za'atar and it is used in everything from salads and meat marinades to pastries and natural flu remedies. This fragrant herb and spice blend is an integral part of Palestinian cuisine.

The word za'atar refers to the plant itself and the velvety heart-shaped leaves can be seen growing all through the mountains in Palestine.

When it comes to the dried za'atar spice mix, the exact combination of herbs and spices varies from maker to maker.

My version is rather sumac-forward, as I adore the exotic tang it brings, and the soft pillowy dough acts as the perfect vessel for these flavours.

I would recommend making a double or triple batch of the spice mix to have on hand in the pantry. It keeps forever and is a gorgeous addition to many a meal.

In the bowl of a stand mixer with the paddle attachment, place the flour, cardamom, yeast, sugar and salt.

With the mixer on low, start slowly pouring in the butter and mix until it is fully incorporated.

Add the yoghurt and vinegar, mixing briefly, followed by the eggs, one by one until they are blended into the mixture.

Swap the paddle attachment over for the dough hook, pour in the water and milk and mix for 10 minutes. The dough should be smooth and elastic; if it is a little on the sticky side add ¼– ½ cup more of flour.

Transfer the dough to an oiled bowl, cover and let rise for 1–1½ hours or until doubled in size. Gently deflate the dough with your palm, cover again and let rest for 15 minutes.

In a small bowl, combine all the Za'atar ingredients.

Preheat the oven to 190°C (375°F) fan-bake. Grease and line a large oven tray.

On a lightly floured bench, roll out the dough to a 45 cm x 30 cm (18 in x 12 in) rectangle about 1 cm (½ in) thick. Mix the za'atar and oil until you have a thick paste and then spread it evenly over the entire piece of dough. Sprinkle the pine nuts evenly over the top.

Starting with the longest edge closest to you, roll into a tight cylinder. Cut each piece into 4 cm (1½ in) rolls; we want about 10–11 rolls. A very sharp knife or sometimes a piece of dental floss is the way to go here; slightly unorthodox I know, but needs must!

Arrange the buns on the prepared tray, 3 cm (1¼ in) apart, shaping

Dough

630 g (1 lb 6 oz) plain flour
½ teaspoon cardamom
14 g (½ oz) instant dried yeast
15 g (½ oz) caster sugar
1½ teaspoons flaky salt
75 g (2¾ oz) butter, melted and cooled
70 g (2½ oz) yoghurt
1 teaspoon white vinegar
2 eggs
125 ml (4 fl oz/½ cup) lukewarm water
125 ml (4 fl oz/½ cup) lukewarm milk

Za'atar

15 g (½ oz) dried oregano
15 g (½ oz) dried thyme
55 g (2 oz) sumac
25 g (1 oz) flaky salt
70 g (2½ oz) white sesame seeds, toasted

Za'atar Filling

150 ml (5 fl oz) olive oil, plus extra for brushing
50 g (1¾ oz) pine nuts, toasted

them as best you can with your hands so they are as round as possible. Gently brush with oil and cover loosely with a tea towel. Let rest for 15 minutes.

When ready to bake, sprinkle 2 tablespoons of water onto the baking tray; this will help create some steam and help the rising. Cook for 15–20 minutes until golden brown.

Remove from the oven and cover again with a tea towel and rest for 10 minutes. This is a great trick to keep them soft and fluffy. Eat warm with extra lashings of good-quality olive oil.

Mushroom and Gruyère Galette

When I was a kid, I used to run away from my mother in the supermarket only to be found in the mushroom bin inhaling raw mushrooms, physically sitting amongst them having an absolute ball. Safe to say, this garnered some very strange looks from fellow shoppers and mild embarrassment for my poor mum!

While I am still prone to snacking on raw mushrooms, this recipe has far surpassed that snack of choice as my new fungi favourite. It's dreamy for breakfast, lunch or dinner.

For the Rough Puff Pastry, combine the flour, salt and butter in the bowl of a food processor. Pulse until the mixture resembles coarse breadcrumbs; we want little chunks of butter. Tip into a large bowl, make a well in the centre, add the water and bring the dough together with your hands. Shape into a rectangle, about 2 cm (¾ in) thick, wrap in cling film and rest in the fridge for 30 minutes.

Turn the dough out onto a lightly floured bench, and roll until it is three times the width, about 20 cm x 50 cm (8 in x 20 in). Try to keep the edges as straight and even as possible if you can. You may see some streaks of butter; don't overwork these. A little bit of marbling is ideal here. Fold the top third of the dough down to the centre, and then the bottom third up and over that. Give the dough a quarter turn to the left or right and then roll out again to three times the length.

Fold as before, wrap in cling film and chill again for 30 minutes.

Repeat this rolling, folding and chilling process twice more and then the pastry will be ready to use.

For the filling, melt the butter in a large deep frypan over a medium-high heat. Add the mushrooms and garlic and sauté until the mushrooms have browned and softened, about 6–8 minutes. Remove from the heat, tip into a large bowl, and allow to cool to room temperature. Stir through all the other ingredients and mix well to combine.

Preheat the oven to 190°C (375°F) fan-bake. Place a baking tray on the middle rack to heat up.

Roll the pastry out on a large and lightly floured sheet of baking paper until it is 5 mm (¼ in) thick, and then trim to form a 26 cm (10½ in) diameter circle.

Spread the mushroom filling evenly over the pastry, leaving a 5 cm (2 in) border all the way around.

Rough Puff Pastry
225 g (8 oz) plain flour
1 teaspoon flaky salt
225 g (8 oz) butter, cold and diced
90 ml (3 fl oz) cold water

Mushroom and Gruyère Filling
70 g (2½ oz) butter
500 g (1 lb 2 oz) mixed mushrooms, sliced (I used portobellos, button and Swiss brown)
5 cloves garlic, finely chopped
200 g (7 oz) ricotta
80 g (2¾ oz) gruyère, grated
1 teaspoon flaky salt
½ teaspoon freshly ground black pepper
25 ml (¾ fl oz) truffle oil, plus extra for serving
10 g (¼ oz) parsley, finely chopped, plus a handful of whole leaves for garnish
1 egg, beaten for egg wash

Fold the edges of the pastry over the mushrooms, pleating as you go; warm the pastry edges up with your fingertips, as the pleating process is far easier when the dough is slightly warm and pliable.

Brush the edges of the pastry with the egg wash and slide the galette on the baking paper onto the heated oven tray.

Bake for 35–45 minutes until the pastry is cooked through, golden and puffed.

Cool on the tray for 5 minutes before carefully transferring to a serving board and drizzling with extra truffle oil.

Mushroom and Gruyère Galette

Turkish Kol Böreği

Zucchinis are up there with my favourite vegetables and they absolutely shine in this dish. For such a simple filling, the final flavour profile is really robust and punchy.

The trick with filo is to make sure you keep it damp; these sheets dry out in record time and it will be impossible to roll and coil them without serious breakages. Keep the sheets under a moist tea towel and only take out the sheets as you need them.

This is delicious served hot or at room temperature with a big dollop of minted yoghurt.

Preheat the oven to 180°C (350°F) fan-bake. Grease and line a 25 cm (10 in) ovenproof frypan.

For the filling, grate the zucchinis and place in a colander. Sprinkle with salt and allow to sit for 10 minutes; this helps draw all the moisture out. Squeeze to get as much liquid out as possible; we don't want any soggy filo happening here.

Heat the oil in a large frypan and sauté the onion, garlic, fennel seeds, chilli flakes and sumac until softened and fragrant; about 6–8 minutes. Add the drained zucchini to the pan and cook for a further 2–3 minutes before removing from the heat. Allow to cool to room temperature.

Gently fold the feta, herbs and zest through the cooled zucchini mixture. Season to taste.

In a medium bowl whisk together the egg, oil and milk until combined. Set aside.

Lay three pieces of filo on top of each other and brush generously with the milk mixture. Place roughly a quarter of the filling in a line following the longest edge nearest you. Gently roll up into a cylinder, brushing the edge with a little more of the milk mixture so it seals firmly. Gently twist the filo into a coil and place in the middle of the prepared baking dish. Brush with the milk mixture once more.

Repeat three more times with the next 9 filo sheets and filling, coiling them around each other in the dish to make a large spiral. Make sure to brush the tops and sides of each coil with the milk mixture; this is also handy if you need to patch up any broken pastry.

For the topping, whisk the egg and oil together in a small bowl and brush all over the pastry before sprinkling with sesame seeds.

Bake for 40–45 minutes until golden brown and crunchy. Cool briefly in the pan before slicing into generous wedges.

3 zucchinis (approximately 500 g/1 lb 2 oz)
1½ teaspoons flaky salt
40 ml (1¼ fl oz) olive oil
1 large red onion, thinly sliced
5 cloves garlic, finely chopped
1 teaspoon fennel seeds
½–1 teaspoon chilli flakes
1 teaspoon sumac
200 g (7 oz) feta, crumbled
¼ cup fresh mint, finely chopped
¼ cup fresh parsley, finely chopped
¼ cup fresh dill, finely chopped
zest of 1 lemon
salt and black pepper, to season

To assemble
1 egg
2 tablespoons olive oil
105 ml (3½ fl oz) milk
12 sheets filo pastry

Sesame Seed Topping
1 egg
2 tablespoons olive oil
30 g (1 oz) sesame seeds

Potato Pie

Imagine creamy potato gratin, encased in a buttery flaky pastry. Carb on carb heaven!

This is a pretty indulgent dish and so incredibly comforting. It's divine eaten piping hot or at room temperature, and also reheats beautifully in the days following.

For the pastry, place the flour and salt in the bowl of a stand mixer. Add half the butter, and with the paddle attachment, mix until the mixture resembles fine breadcrumbs. This can also be done in a food processor.

Add the remaining butter and water and mix again until the dough comes together. Tip out onto a lightly floured surface, divide the dough into two equal pieces and form into balls.

Press each piece of dough to flatten into discs, about 2 cm (¾ in) thick, wrap separately in cling film and refrigerate for 1 hour.

For the filling, slice the potatoes as thin as possible using either a very sharp knife or a mandoline.

Add to a large bowl with all the remaining ingredients and toss to combine; you want every slice of potato nicely coated and all the seasoning well distributed.

Preheat the oven to 200°C (400°F) fan-bake.

To assemble the tart, roll out each of the pastry discs to 28 cm (11¼ in) diameter rounds. Line a 23 cm (9 in) fluted tart tin with one of the discs, ensuring the sides are nice and snug, leaving a 2 cm (¾ in) overhang.

Add the potatoes in even layers, making sure you get every little bit of the crème fraiche in there, before topping with the second pastry round. Using a small knife, trim the excess dough and crimp all around the edges so the delicious filling is sealed in there.

Make a few small slits in the dough to allow some of the steam to escape and place the tart on a large baking tray.

Mix the egg yolk and cream in a small bowl, and brush generously over the top of the pie.

Bake for 10 minutes before reducing the temperature to 175°C (335°F) fan-bake and cooking for a further 1¼–1½ hours. The top should be golden brown and a skewer should go through the potatoes easily.

Cool in the tin for 10 minutes before serving.

Plain Pastry

250 g (9 oz) plain flour
½ teaspoon salt
225 g (8 oz) butter, cold and diced
125 ml (4 fl oz/½ cup) cold water

Potato Filling

1 kg (2 lb 4 oz) yellow flesh potatoes
310 g (11 oz) crème fraiche
30 g (1 oz) wholegrain mustard
1 tablespoon flaky salt
½ teaspoon black pepper
pinch of grated nutmeg
4 cloves garlic, finely chopped
2 teaspoons picked rosemary leaves, finely chopped
2 teaspoons picked thyme leaves, finely chopped

Egg wash

1 egg yolk
1 tablespoon cream

Fatayers

Fatayers are traditional Lebanese pastries which are essentially the Middle Eastern version of the Greek classic spanakopita.

There are a few different filling options that are common, including a mixture of cheeses or minced lamb, but my personal favourite is this simple (yet very effective) spinach and sumac number. The sumac is essential and generous here, giving the filling a gorgeous tang with a little hint of citrus fruitiness.

This is a recipe where frozen spinach is preferred over its fresh counterpart as we all know spinach is notorious for cooking down to nothing. It's very important that the spinach is as dry as possible before it is mixed with the other ingredients, as soggy dough is no one's friend.

The filling can be made a day in advance and actually benefits from sitting in the fridge overnight, allowing the flavours to really develop.

For the dough, combine all the ingredients in the bowl of a stand mixer with the dough hook attachment. Mix for 10 minutes until smooth and elastic.

Transfer to an oiled bowl, cover and allow to prove for 1 hour or until doubled in size.

Meanwhile for the filling, combine all the ingredients in a medium bowl, mixing well to combine. Season to taste.

Preheat the oven to 175°C (335°F) fan-bake. Grease and line two large oven trays.

When the dough has doubled in size, tip out onto a floured surface and divide into 12 pieces, weighing approximately 70 g (2½ oz) each.

Working with one piece of dough at a time, roll out into a rectangle, measuring 12 cm (4½ in) long and 10 cm (4 in) wide. Spoon about 60 g (2¼ oz) of filling into the centre of the dough and spread out evenly, leaving a 1 cm (½ in) border all the way around. Pinch the ends together and fold up the sides; you're looking to create an almost canoe-like shape.

Repeat this process with the remaining dough and filling and place all the fatayers on the prepared baking trays.

Brush each fatayer with oil and sprinkle with a little extra flaky salt.

Bake for 20–25 minutes until golden brown and crisped. Allow to cool for 5–10 minutes before serving.

Dough
500 g (1 lb 2 oz) plain flour
7 g (¼ oz) instant dried yeast
6 g (⅛ oz) brown sugar
6 g (⅛ oz) flaky salt
1 tablespoon olive oil
300 ml (10½ fl oz) lukewarm water

Spinach and Sumac Filling
400 g (14 oz) frozen spinach, thawed, squeezed as dry as possible and roughly chopped
1 teaspoon flaky salt, plus extra for sprinkling
50 g (1¾ oz) pine nuts, toasted and roughly chopped
12 g (¼ oz) sumac
5 g (⅛ oz) Aleppo chilli flakes
1 red onion (about 150 g/ 5½ oz), finely chopped
40 ml (1¼ fl oz) pomegranate molasses
2 tablespoons olive oil, plus extra for brushing
zest of 1 lemon
8 g (¼ oz) mint leaves, thinly sliced
10 g (¼ oz) Italian parsley, finely chopped
300 g (10½ oz) feta, crumbled

Cavolo Nero and Mozzarella Foldovers

Cavolo nero, also known as black kale, originates from Italy. It has a slightly lighter and sweeter taste than its curly counterpart.

This foldover makes for a gorgeous brunch or lunch and for a yeasted dough, it's very quick to put together. You can play around with the cheeses, but I've stuck to the Italian brief; since when has buffalo mozzarella been a bad idea?

For the dough, combine all the ingredients in the bowl of a stand mixer and, with the dough hook attached, mix on a low speed for 5 minutes before increasing to a medium speed and mixing for a further 5 minutes. The dough should look quite soft and be elastic and stretchy. Transfer to an oiled bowl, cover and let rise for about 45 minutes or until it has doubled in size.

For the filling, in a large frypan, heat the oil and sauté the shallot, garlic and chilli flakes for 7–8 minutes over a low-medium heat. Add in the zest and juice along with the cavolo nero and stir until the leaves have softened and wilted slightly. Transfer to a large bowl and allow to cool to room temperature before stirring through the remaining ingredients. Season to taste with flaky salt and pepper.

Roll the dough onto a lightly floured surface and gently pat into a 30 cm x 20 cm (12 in x 8 in) rectangle. Fold the dough in half, then half again before popping in the bowl for a second prove; about 30 minutes.

Turn the dough out once again onto the floured surface and roll into the same-sized rectangle. You will want to use a liberal amount of flour here as the dough can be a little on the sticky side.

Spread the filling evenly over two-thirds of the dough, leaving the remaining third bare. Fold the bare part of the dough over half the filling, and then fold again so everything is encased.

Flour the top and gently pat it out so the top is flat and even. The width should be roughly 15 cm (6 in).

Cover loosely with cling film and let sit for 10 minutes.

Preheat the oven to 180°C (350°F) fan-bake. Grease and line a large baking tray.

Using a sharp knife or pizza cutter, cut the dough in half lengthways and then across the rows to form 10 even pieces. Carefully transfer the foldovers to the prepared baking tray for their final 10 minutes prove.

Bake for about 20–25 minutes until golden and crisped; some of the filling may spill out a little, but to be honest, those oozy crispy bits are kind of the best part! Cool momentarily on a wire rack before scoffing.

Dough

450 g (1 lb) plain flour
2 teaspoons caster sugar
2 teaspoons flaky salt
1 teaspoon freshly ground black pepper
10 g (¼ oz) instant dried yeast
300 ml (10½ fl oz) lukewarm water
1 tablespoon olive oil

Cavolo Nero and Mozzarella Filling

¼ cup olive oil
1 shallot, finely chopped
4 cloves garlic, finely chopped
1 teaspoon chilli flakes
zest of 2 lemons
juice of 1 lemon
200 g (7 oz) cavolo nero, central stem removed and leaves finely shredded
250 g (9 oz) buffalo mozzarella, drained and coarsely torn
50 g (1¾ oz) Pecorino Romano, grated
70 g (2½ oz) pine nuts, toasted
20 g (¾ oz) basil leaves, thinly sliced
20 g (¾ oz) parsley, finely chopped

Jerusalem Bagels

These gorgeous golden ovals are derived from the the ka'ak bread ring found throughout the Middle East. They are famously sold by street vendors in the streets of Old Jerusalem, which is where I happily stumbled across them for the first time.

They are far less dense than the bagels most people know and are simply baked; no boiling involved.

Soft and airy, arguably the best part about them is the gorgeously salty-sweet flavour that comes from the honeyed sesame topping.

Jerusalem bagels are best eaten on the day of making. If you can refrain from polishing off the whole batch while still warm, I applaud your willpower.

To make the dough, combine all the ingredients in the bowl of a stand mixer with the dough hook attached. Knead for 10 minutes on a low speed until it is smooth and elastic. Shape the dough into a ball and transfer to an oiled bowl, cover with cling film and allow to prove until doubled in size; about 1 hour.

Grease and line two oven trays.

Tip the risen dough out onto a lightly floured bench and divide into 6 equal pieces; I often weigh them out at this point. They should be roughly 150 g (5½ oz) each.

Working with one ball of dough at a time, roll out into 45 cm (18 in) long strands. Squeeze the ends together and gently stretch the dough until you have an elongated oval shape. If the dough doesn't stretch too easily at first, let it rest for a couple of minutes before giving it another pull. You want the bagels nice and long; about 25 cm (10 in).

Place the bagels on the prepared trays, cover with cling film and let rest for another hour. They won't expand greatly here, but they should puff up a little.

Preheat the oven to 180°C (350°F) fan-bake.

For the topping, in a small bowl, mix together the honey and water. Brush each bagel liberally with this mixture before sprinkling all over with the sesame seeds. Be generous here. Sprinkle with sea salt.

Bake in the oven for 20–25 minutes until golden brown.

Transfer to a wire rack and cover with a tea towel for 5 minutes; this helps keep the bread nice and soft.

Dough
500 g (1 lb 2 oz) plain flour
300 ml (10½ fl oz) room temperature water
7 g (¼ oz) instant dried yeast
60 g (2¼ oz) milk powder
50 g (1¾ oz) caster sugar
15 g (½ oz) fine salt
20 ml (¾ fl oz) extra virgin olive oil

Honey Topping
30 g (1 oz) runny honey
1 tablespoon water
100 g (3½ oz) white sesame seeds, toasted
sea salt, for sprinkling

Bazlama

Bazlama is a Turkish flatbread, not overly dissimilar to naan, and is traditionally cooked on an outdoor wood fire. It is often referred to as 'village bread' and can be seen for sale in stands at most Turkish markets.

This bread is made using yoghurt, which gives the dough a lovely tang in flavour and an incredibly tender texture. Bazlama is a very low-maintenance bread when it comes to the actual elbow grease required. There are only mere minutes of kneading involved and a very short resting time, so it is the perfect recipe for those who are time-poor or just hungry!

It makes for a gorgeous addition to any mezze platter, as well as a wonderful vessel for dips.

12 g (¼ oz) instant dried yeast
12 g (¼ oz) caster sugar
295 ml (10 fl oz) water
185 g (6½ oz) Greek yoghurt
2 tablespoons olive oil
12 g (¼ oz) salt
470 g (1 lb ½ oz) plain flour
¼ cup parsley, chopped
extra virgin olive oil, for brushing

Combine the yeast, sugar and water in a medium bowl, stir well and allow to sit for 5–10 minutes until foamy.

Whisk in the yoghurt, oil and salt.

Add the flour and parsley and bring together with your hands before tipping out onto a lightly floured bench. Knead for 3–4 minutes until the dough is no longer sticky and it springs back when lightly pressed. Divide the dough into 10 equal pieces, sprinkle lightly with flour, then cover with a clean tea towel. Allow to rest for 15 minutes.

Preheat a medium pan to a medium heat. While the pan is heating, roll one of the dough portions into a 16 cm (6¼ in) round. Brush the surface lightly with the oil.

When the pan is nearly smoking hot, place the flatbread in, oiled side down. Lightly brush the top surface with oil. Allow to the flatbread to cook for 60–90 seconds, until the top surface is covered with bubbles and the underside is golden around the edges.

Flip over and cook for another 60–90 seconds until a few small golden spots appear. Be mindful not to overcook on the second side. Repeat the rolling, oiling and frying with the remaining dough, stacking the cooked flatbreads in a tea towel so they steam a little and retain their softness.

Bazlama is best eaten on the day of making.

Acknowledgements

To my family; my mum, dad, brother Max and sister-in-law Amy. I hit the jackpot with my family and feel immensely lucky that they are mine. The unwavering support, outrageously loud enthusiasm, and endless love; you are the best people I know.

My girlfriends, who are more like sisters; Ella, Hannah, Fran, Maxine, Claire, Anna, Neen, Rosa. The most special, inspiring group of women that I feel so proud to know.

Photographer Mel Jenkins and Food Stylist Jo Bridgford; it was both a treat and a privilege to work with you both. Two hugely talented, warm, hilariously funny women. We bonded from day one and I adore you both.

Peter and Al; the best bosses anyone could ask for. Thank you for being so encouraging throughout this whole process. You have allowed me so much creative freedom in your kitchen and your support has meant the world to me.

Jenny; my profound thanks for giving me this opportunity and for your advice and encouragement throughout the whole process. This would not have happened without you and I feel so lucky to have worked alongside you and your talented team at Allen & Unwin.

Allen & Unwin
Level 2, 10 College Hill
Auckland 1011, New Zealand
Phone: (64 9) 377 3800

Email: info@allenandunwin.com
Web: www.allenandunwin.co.nz

83 Alexander Street
Crows Nest NSW 2065, Australia
Phone: (61 2) 8425 0100

A catalogue record for this book is available
from the National Library of New Zealand

ISBN 978 1 99100 620 2

Design by Kate Barraclough

Set in Crake Bold and Tiempos Text
Printed and bound in China by C & C Printing Co., Ltd.
10 9 8 7 6 5 4 3 2 1

FSC
www.fsc.org
MIX
Paper | Supporting
responsible forestry
FSC® C008047